# RITUAL UNBOUND

# RITUAL UNBOUND

## Reading Sacrifice in Modernist Fiction

Thomas J. Cousineau

**DELAWARE**

Newark: University of Delaware Press

Associated University Presses
2010 Eastpark Boulevard
Cranbury, NJ 08512

The paper used in this publication meets the requirements of the American National Standard for Permanence of Paper for Printed Library Materials Z39.48–1984.

Library of Congress Cataloging-in-Publication Data

Cousineau, Thomas.
Ritual unbound : reading sacrifice in modernist fiction / Thomas J. Cousineau.
    p. cm.
Includes bibliographical references (p.  ) and index.
ISBN 0-87413-851-5 (alk. paper)
1. English fiction—20th century—History and criticism. 2. Scapegoat in literature. 3. Fitzgerald, F. Scott (Francis Scott), 1896-1940. Great Gatsby. 4. Woolf, Virginia, 1882-1941. To the lighthouse. 5. Conrad, Joseph, 1857-1924. Heart of darkness. 6. James, Henry, 1843-1916. Turn of the screw. 7. Ford, Ford Madox, 1873-1939. Good soldier. *. Modernism (Literature)—Great Britain. 9. Modernism (Literature)—United States. 10. Rites and ceremonies in literature. 11. Sacrifice in literature. I. Title.
PR888. S32C68 2004
823'.912093552—dc22

                                                                    2003023516

*For Matthew and Laure*

We cannot do without the scapegoat. His existence is a biological necessity for each one of us. Someone must pay the price of our faults and our failings. If we were to think of ourselves as solely responsible, what complications, what additional tortures this would involve. To be given a *clear conscience* is all that we ask, and the scapegoat does this for us.

Blaming ourselves for everything requires a superhuman effort. When we do this, however, we sense that we are drawing near to the truth. Alas, this makes us, not more modest, but more proud.

— E. M. Cioran, *Cahiers 1957–72*

# Contents

# Acknowledgments

THIS BOOK IS A LONG-MEDITATED RESPONSE AS WELL AS A TRIBUTE TO Thomas Hanzo and to the seminar on modernist fiction that he taught at the University of California at Davis in the 1960s. During the intervening years, students in my own modernist classes at Washington College and at the University of Paris have provided me with essential guidance of a quite different sort. I was also helped along the way by the encouraging reactions to early drafts of the manuscript offered to me by several friends and colleagues, including Calla Denjoy, Richard DeProspo, Richard Harwood, Ellen Lévy, Robert Mooney, Margaret Ann O'Connor, Stephen Severn, Michelle Sommers, and Joseph and Claire Whitehill. Keith Carabine and John Vernon gave me detailed critiques of several chapters that led to significant revisions. My wife Diane was with me as always. Washington College has generously supported my work through timely awards of faculty-enchancement grants. I wish lastly to thank Christine Retz and Kathleen Cioffi of Associated University Presses for their expert supervision of the final stages of publication.

Earlier versions of chapters 2 and 4 appeared, respectively, in "*Heart of Darkness*: The Outsider Demystified," *Conradiana* 30, no. 2:140–51, and "*The Great Gatsby*: Romance or Holocaust?," *Contagion* 8:21–35. My thanks to the editors for their permission to include this work here.

# RITUAL
# UNBOUND

# Introduction:
# From Ritual to Modernism

In *FROM RITUAL TO ROMANCE,* WHOSE ROLE IN INSPIRING T. S. ELIOT'S
*The Waste Land* is well known, Jessie Weston argued that medieval
grail legends, although clearly based on ancient vegetation rituals,
had largely subordinated these primitive sources to strikingly new literary purposes. Using Chrétien de Troyes's *Percival* as her example,
Weston pointed to the fact that its author had integrated his *ancient*
ritual materials into a work that was primarily about the exploits of a
*medieval* knight: "We have here passed completely and entirely into
the land of romance, the doors of the Temple are closed behind us.
It is the story of Perceval li Gallois, not the Ritual of the Grail, which
fills the stage" (161–62).

A similar transformation may be observed in modernist fiction,
which frequently features a protagonist beneath whose ostensibly realistic adventures we detect perceptible mythic resonances.[1] On the
one hand, we find in these novels the modernist equivalent of Percival: solitary figures who are variously named "the governess," "Edward Ashburnham," "Kurtz," "Gatsby," or "Lily Briscoe." Each of these
figures, in obedience to the conventions of novelistic realism, is
placed in a reasonably plausible story that is not overtly related to
primitive rituals. At the same time, however, the authors of these
novels often disturb their realistic surfaces with incongruous details
that suddenly allow us to glimpse their mythic substrata. Invariably,
this involves the revelation of a sacrificial ritual directed against a
protagonist who has been made vulnerable by his or her solitude.
Thus, the governess in *The Turn of the Screw* will refer to herself as an

15

"expiatory victim," and Nick Carraway will characterize Gatsby's murder as a "holocaust."

This susceptibility of literary works to readings that emphasize either the psychology of a particular individual or the sacrificial practices of a community is not, to be sure, the special preserve of modernist fiction. In fact, one of the most interesting cases of this intersection occurs in Sophocles' classical tragedy, *Oedipus the King*. Sigmund Freud had speculated that, for a modern audience, the explanation of the continued power of this ancient play must be its appeal to our unconscious "Oedipal" impulses. For Freud, the fascination of Sophocles' play rests with the eponymous hero's violation of the prohibitions against parricide and incest. The desires that Oedipus acts out are, according to this hypothesis, precisely those that spectators of the play must repress in order to gain entry into the realm of civilized existence.

In *Violence and the Sacred*, René Girard offered, in contrast to Freud, a reading of *Oedipus the King* that emphatically displaced attention away from the repressed incestuous and parricidal desires that are enacted by the *individual* figure of Oedipus himself and underlined, rather, the *communal* practice of scapegoating that the play itself enacts. For Girard, the designation of Oedipus as *solely* responsible for the plague—an act that serves to legitimize his expulsion from the community—explains the power of the play to reveal, not the unconscious desires of the individual members of its audience, but the mystifying resort to scapegoats to which their community is prone. In his revision of the Freudian reading, Girard thus emphasized actual communal practices rather than the psychology of a particular individual.[2]

Unlike *Oedipus the King*, however, which most readers interpret as justifying Oedipus's expulsion from Thebes, modernist works come unambiguously to the defense of their protagonists, whom they invariably regard as victims of societal prejudices. For this reason, as William Johnsen has cogently argued, the modernist use of ritual elements cannot be interpreted as simply an act of recovery. Rather, it amounts to a profoundly critical act, "an archeological dis-covery of the roots of all human societies in violent sacrifice" (in Segal, *Theories of Myth*, 129). Ritual is shown by such works not merely to be an ancient, foundational process, but one whose presuppositions cannot survive examination by the rational intellect. Similarly, in his commentary on T. S. Eliot's use of Weston's study of ritual, G. M. Jones stresses Eliot's *critically engaged* relationship with his mythic materials: "Myth in the hands of the artist is a different thing from myth in the hands of the primitive thinker. The primitive thinker is at the mercy of a form of consciousness from which he cannot escape. Not so the artist. His thinking is not helplessly dominated by myth; he stands outside it and contemplates it as a form of thought" (59). Indeed, many of the masterpieces of literary modernism—one thinks immediately, along with *The Waste Land,* of James Joyce's *Ulysses* and William Faulkner's *Light in August*—express their authors' fundamental rejection of the scapegoating practices that appear in them.[3]

The novels that I have chosen for this study are quintessentially modernist in their defense of a solitary protagonist who has become the target of communal violence. At the same time, however, they possess certain features that make of them a distinctive subgroup within modernist fiction. To begin with, the sacrificial rituals that we find in these novels are not so much observable communal practices as they are hypothetical constructions that have been projected upon the stories by their narrators. When, for example, the governess in *The Turn of the Screw* refers to herself as an "expiatory victim," this designation does not have the same objective validity as it does when, for example, applied to the killing of Joe Christmas in *Light in August.* Likewise, when Nick Carraway refers to Gatsby's death as a "holocaust," we recognize in his choice of this term his desire to construct a sacrificial scene that does not apply in an obvious and unarguable way to the actual circumstances of Gatsby's death. For this reason, the victimization that we find here seems highly speculative and even, perhaps, self-serving.[4]

In a related way, the distinction between accepting or rejecting scapegoating does not apply to these novels as unproblematically as it does to other modernist masterpieces. Although committed to the demystification of atavistic practices, their narrators tend to defend the designated victims in ways that ironically produce a *remystification* of sacrifice.[5] While taking the side of these victims against their persecutors, they often encourage the community of readers assembled around them to direct its own scapegoating impulses against other targeted figures. As a result, they create a highly unstable relationship between the scapegoat, the community that persecutes him, and the narrator that comes to his defense. The moral interest of

these works lies–not in the defense of the victim or even in the im-
puting of blame to the fictional community–but in the revelation of
the complicity that makes of ourselves as readers an all-too-real
community whose own scapegoating impulses have been successfully
enlisted in the narrator's cause. In this way, they give especially pre-
scient expression to a fundamental contradiction of our own historical period. On the one hand, we recognize the injustice of perse-
cuting victims in whose guilt we can no longer plausibly believe; on
the other hand, we cannot imagine how to create a human community that does not have its scapegoats.

Finally, each of these novels is constructed in such a way as to create an implicit contrast between the narrator's merely *ostensible* demystification of scapegoating, which is contaminated by an unpurged
mythic residue, and the *genuine* demystification undertaken—to the
degree that we succeed in seeing beyond the distorting interference
of the narrator—by the events of the novel. The pattern created by
these events—which constitutes a form of order not dependent
upon the expulsion of a sacrificial victim—serves throughout the
novels themselves as a silent challenge to the scapegoating discourse
of the narrator. The aesthetic form of each novel proposes, in effect,
an *imaginary* solution to the intractable problem of creating, in the
*real* world, a non-sacrificial community.

The placing of a solitary protagonist against the background of a
sacrificial subtext may be readily observed in Henry James's *The Turn
of the Screw*. James's novella appears, on the one hand, to focus attention on the inner, subjective world of the young governess as she
struggles to protect her charges from the malign purposes of two
ghosts, who have themselves often been interpreted as projections of
her own psychological complexes. So inviting is a psychological interpretation of James's tale that the most famous reading that it has
received, Edmund Wilson's in "The Ambiguity of Henry James," con-
fidently asserts that the key to its understanding lies in our recognizing that the presumed events of the story itself are, in fact, the
fantasies of a "frustrated middle-class spinster" (in Esch and Warren,
*Turn of the Screw*, 173).

James does, however, invest both the main story and the frame tale with details that, while having little to do with the private fantasies of his young governess, significantly point our attention toward the underlying ritual and communal aspects of his story. The novella itself begins, for example, not with the solitary governess's narrative, but with a convivial group of adults sitting by a ceremonial fire, on a sacred occasion (Christmas Eve) and taking pleasure in stories in which children are sacrificed, at least metaphorically, by the suffering that they undergo in their ghost stories. The governess will, in turn, decisively shift her otherwise solitary and private experiences at Bly to the public arena when she attributes to herself a sacrificial role. Even more incongruously (considering her own admission that she has never been to a theater) she will add to this public dimension by sprinkling her narrative with theatrical metaphors, as when she compares Bly in the autumn to "a theater after the performance—all strewn with crumpled playbills" (211)[6] or describes as "the last jerk of the curtain" (189) her request that Mrs. Grose clarify her remark about Miles.

At such moments as these, James abandons the requirements of verisimilitude in order to imbue the governess's private experience with a communal dimension that it would otherwise lack. James himself explicitly alluded to the relevance of public rituals to his tale when he remarked in his preface that, "Peter Quint and Miss Jessel are not 'ghosts' at all, as we know the ghost, but goblins, elves, imps, demons as loosely constructed as those of *the old trials for witchcraft*" (41; my emphasis). Following James's lead, several recent readings of *The Turn of the Screw* have pointed to his horrified reaction to the trial and subsequent punishment of Oscar Wilde as an important subtext. Such interpretations take us very far indeed from the sexual frustrations of a spinster as an explanatory key to events in the novella. They tend, rather, to contextualize it in relation to the self-protective acts of ritual punishment to which both individuals and communities have recourse.

Similarly, Joseph Conrad's *Heart of Darkness* is, on the one hand, the story of the psychological impact upon Marlow of his journey up the Congo River and, in particular, his encounter with Kurtz. The preeminence of psychological considerations is conveyed by the doctor's remark to Marlow, before he undertakes his journey, that the "changes take place inside" (27)[7] as well as by the impressionistic techniques that vividly register Marlow's subjective experiences. A psychoanalytical interpretation of major events is authorized by the portrayal of the jungle as a maternal figure that exercises an irresistible, yet ultimately destructive, power over the "civilized" Europeans who wander into it, by Marlow's projection of paternal traits upon Kurtz, and by the profoundly transgressive quality of Kurtz's violation of taboos as well as the dream of recapturing the infantile fantasy of omnipotence that they serve. Coexisting with this psychological focus, however, is the novel's equally important concern with the representation of atavistic communal practices that involve the sacrifice of a designated individual, the most obvious example of which is the "unspeakable practices" of which Marlow speaks. Less violent, although arguably more pervasive, forms of ritual exclusion also appear in the novel. Thus, the members of the company affirm their solidarity through the judgment whereby they designate Kurtz as a pariah, and Marlow constructs a community of civilized white males by excluding black Africans and European women.

Ford Madox Ford creates a similarly dual perspective in *The Good Soldier.* The emotional life of Edward Ashburnham, and the rendering of a hypocritical society that frustrates normal sexual drives is obviously a primary center of interest for Dowell, who is clearly fascinated by the "raging stallion forever neighing after his neighbour's womenkind" (14)[8] that he discovers in Edward. The adoption of a first-person narrative technique assures, in turn, that we will become intimately acquainted with myriad details of Dowell's own subjective response to the events that he is narrating. At the same time, however, we detect, beneath the realistically drawn surface of this psychological novel, allusions to atavistic sacrificial practices, particularly in Dowell's portrayal of Edward as the innocent victim of a persecution-minded community whose determination to punish him is embodied in its most virulent form by the major female characters in the novel.

*The Great Gatsby* is likewise constructed around two competing centers of attention. On the one hand, it is the story of Gatsby's longing to recapture the romantic experiences that he shared with Daisy several years earlier in Louisville. An "Oedipal" pattern, in the sense given to this expression by Freud, can be readily seen in Gatsby's desire to conquer a formidable male rival and to possess a forbidden woman, in whose company "he could suck on the pap of life, gulp down the incomparable milk of wonder" (117).[9] As in *The Good Soldier*, the psychological interest of the story will be divided between the portrayal of Gatsby's own subjective dream and the personal response, both admiring and critical, that this evokes in Nick Carraway. Although he clearly builds his novel around intimate personal relationships, however, Fitzgerald also organizes its principal events with a view toward the sacrificial altar upon which Gatsby will ultimately die. Gatsby is literally killed, to be sure, in his swimming pool by the solitary figure of George Wilson, who mistakenly blames him for the killing of his wife. Nick, however, refers to Gatsby's death as a "holocaust," a word that, as I shall argue in detail later, is no mere malapropism but, rather, a revelatory choice of vocabulary that connects with an entire network of details that creates throughout the novel an ambiguous image of Gatsby as, on the one hand, a romantic hero and, on the other, a sacrificial victim.

Like these preceding novels, *To The Lighthouse* is thoroughly modernist in its preoccupation with the subjective experience of its protagonists, especially Mr. and Mrs. Ramsay and Lily Briscoe. This psychological emphasis is maintained, and perhaps even reinforced, throughout the third and final section, which offers a concentrated focus on Lily's subjective impressions as she responds, at first, to the irritating intrusion upon her personal space by Mr. Ramsay and, later, to the challenge of completing her long- contemplated painting. Throughout the novel, Woolf underlines the specifically familial dimension of Lily's progress toward eventual self-affirmation, with Mrs. Ramsay playing the role of a substitute mother who wants Lily to find fulfillment in matrimony and Mr. Ramsay serving as the patriarchal father who embodies the social norms that would exclude her from full participation in those forms of productive cultural activity that have traditionally been reserved for men.

The parallel portrayal of a community that resorts to exclusionary, sacrificial practices in order to guarantee its solidarity is already at work in the tacit assumption that Lily, as a woman, should not intrude upon a male preserve. This foundational example of exclusion is then echoed in several of the novel's principal episodes. Thus, at the beginning of *To the Lighthouse,* Woolf shows the Ramsay children banding together in their shared disdain for Charles Tansley. At the dinner party, the decisive, integrating moment that draws together the otherwise disparate and isolated guests occurs when the lighting of the candles creates a sense of solidarity that opposes all of them to the "fluidity out there" (97).[10] In a similar way, the restoration of order that occurs at the end of the transitional "Time Passes" section will be made possible by the activity of working-class people who are otherwise excluded from participation in the social and cultural activities of the Ramsays and their guests. Finally, the novel clearly indicates that Lily's successful completion of her painting depends upon the successive exclusions involved, first, in the death of Mrs. Ramsay, and, second, in Mr. Ramsay's departure for the lighthouse.

In *Things Hidden Since the Foundation of the World*, Girard suggests that the Hebrew Bible, the Gospels, Greek tragedy, and the plays of Shakespeare are characterized, in contrast to what he calls "persecution narratives," by their readiness to come to the defense of an unjustly persecuted victim. He defines myth negatively as "a text that has been falsified by the belief of the executioners in the guiltiness of their victim." He further argues that myths characteristically "incorporate the point of view of the community that has been reconciled to itself by the collective murder and is unanimously convinced that this event was a legitimate and sacred action, desired by God himself, which could not conceivably be repudiated, criticized, or analyzed" (150). Already in Greek tragedy, however, Girard detects signs of the nascent effort to demystify the communal delusions that are embodied in myth. This process gains momentum in the Hebrew Bible (in which the prophets explicitly reject sacrificial rituals), reaches its culmination in the Gospels, which proclaim the innocence of the sacrificial victim in the person of Christ, and is echoed in modern novels, which, like their classic predecessors, demystify the atavistic beliefs that had heretofore served to justify the persecutory instincts of the community.

The major critical studies of scapegoating in modern novels have been largely concerned with formulating a response to the crucial question that Girard sets forth in *The Scapegoat:*

> Before invoking the scapegoat in connection with a text we must first ask whether we are dealing with a scapegoat *of* the text (the hidden structural principle) or a scapegoat *in* the

text (the clearly visible theme). Only in the first case can the text be defined as one of persecution, entirely subjected to the representation of persecution from the standpoint of the persecutor. This text is controlled by the effect of a scapegoat it does not acknowledge. In the second case, on the contrary, the text acknowledges the scapegoat effect which does not control it. Not only is this text no longer a persecution text, but it even reveals the truth of the persecution. (119)

In responding to this question, John Vickery argues that the skeptical treatment of ritual that one finds already in Greek tragedy is reborn in a particularly powerful way in the novels of D. H. Lawrence, William Faulkner, James Baldwin, Fyodor Dostoyevski, and Jean Genet. He finds in Yakov Bok, the hero of Bernard Malamud's *The Fixer, a* character who "emerges with a deeply integrated conviction born of experience that explodes the underlying premise of the scapegoat and his ritual" (in McCune, Orbison, and Withim, *Binding of Proteus,* 276). He further suggests that, in the novel itself, "the principle of vicarious suffering . . . is denied by its moral and psychological antithesis, the principle of individual human responsibility" (277). Laura Barge explicitly adopts the Girardian paradigm in her argument that the scapegoat himself can be classified along a spectrum defined at one extreme as "purely mythical" (in which the sacrificial pattern is not subjected to criticism) and at the other as "purely non-mythical" (in which it is absolutely denounced). She adds, however, a qualification that has affinities with my own approach when she locates, between these extremes, examples that, whether tending toward the mythical or the non-mythical, contain impurities that produce a mixed, incomplete form of revelation.

Applying this paradigm to her analysis of Ralph Ellison's *The Invisible Man,* Barge notes the tension between Ellison's authorial condemnation of scapegoating and the protagonist's initial obliviousness to it. She then describes the narrative movement as leading to a moral discovery whereby "the protagonist becomes fully aware of the unjust forces allied against him and joins the author and reader in a textual experience that convincingly discloses the evil of racial victimization in twentieth-century America" ("René Girard's Categories," 258). Barge notes another ironic representation of this process of disclosure in Kate Chopin's short story, "Désirée's Baby," in which the protagonist "never realizes either the falsity or the in-

justice of the judgments against her, though we as readers, in response to Chopin's skill in rendering irony, pass severe judgment
not only on Armand but also on the society that supports his preju-
dicial rage" (258). As we shall eventually see, our novels create even
further ironies that will require additional refinements of Girard's
master model of the movement from concealment to disclosure.
The actual victimization to which Barge rightly calls attention will
become rather more hypothetical, and the salient question will be
the degree to which the protagonists (as well as their readers) recognize their roles, not as *victims*, but as *perpetrators* of new forms of
persecution.

In *Expulsion in the Nineteenth-Century Novel,* which offers one of the
most impressive responses to Girard's question, Michiel Heyns demonstrates that the five realistic novels that he analyzes–which are generally reputed to endorse the historical practice of scapegoating and
to defend essentially conservative attitudes—actually create an op-
positional narrative whose values are more progressive. Although
Heyns's focus is on nineteenth-century realistic fiction, his book is a
rich and invaluable source of insights regarding modernist fiction as
well. Adopting specifically Girardian terminology in his analysis of
Jane Austen's *Mansfield Park,* Heyns argues that we must distinguish
the scapegoat *in* the text from the scapegoat *of* the text, a process
that will allow us to distinguish usefully between the socially conservative community within the novel itself and the more enlightened
community of readers to whose progressive instincts Austen makes
an implicit appeal.

In a similar way, Heyns's analysis of Dickens's *Our Mutual Friend*
leads him to conclude that this novel projects, in the form of its potential readers, a "community with its own implicit rules and regulations, its conditions of membership, often opposed to those of the
society depicted in the novel" (*Expulsion,* 22). In supporting this
idea, he points to ways in which Dickens himself undermines the legitimacy of scapegoating even as he constructs a plot that appears to
justify ritualized exclusions. This leads him to conclude that the
scapegoats that appear in Dickens's novels embody qualities that the
author endorses even though he "cannot afford to sanction" them
(28). Heyns notes a similar ambivalence in the work of George Eliot,
a writer in whom he detects a conflict between "the conscious conservative moralist" and "the subconscious subversive" (31). *Daniel*

*Deronda* exemplifies his central argument that "the techniques and forms of realist representation, adapted to an ethical intention, both necessitate and militate against scapegoating" (39). As we shall eventually see, however, the dichotomies that Heyns invokes here are neatly reversed in the novels that I have chosen for this study. The "conscious" intentions of these novels are *subversive*, while their "subconscious" countermovement is *conservative*. They demonstrate that an attitude of conscious rejection of scapegoating does not preclude—and, in fact, may even necessitate—its restoration, albeit in forms that are highly resistant to detection. Likewise, Heyns's analysis of the progressive tendencies of modernist fiction, represented by the novels of Joseph Conrad and Henry James, will eventually require qualification.

Heyns is nonetheless unquestionably right in asserting that the self-consciousness characteristic of modernist fiction is the key to its potentially liberating resolution of the deadlock between endorsement and repudiation of scapegoating to which realistic fiction seems ineluctably bound. The fact that scapegoating becomes the subject *of* such fiction rather than a structural element *in* it produces the critical movement from the mythical to the non-mythical representation of the scapegoat. In pursuing this insight, Heyns contests the assumption that Henry James's *The Golden Bowl* condones the foundational lies of a society "in the interests of the civilization that it tries to preserve and protect" (48). Against this traditional reading he contends that James's novel actually "exposes the coercive and manipulative potential of 'morality' itself, that is, of the moral structures a society erects for its own protection and the exclusion of threats to its power" (48).

In her *The Science of Sacrifice: American Literature and Modern Social Theory*, Susan L. Mizruchi offers a detailed analysis of James *The Awkward Age* that echoes in certain respects Heyns's analysis of *The Golden Bowl*, particularly with respect to the tension between conservative acceptance and progressivist rejection of scapegoating. Mizruchi reads this novel as the literary expression of the powerful impact made on James by his encountering as a young man Henry Holman Hunt's painting, *The Scapegoat*. Finding in its opening pages allusions to ritual purification in which "James depicts watery rites, the symbolic cleansing designed to rid a community of pollution" (193), Mizruchi argues that the novel itself "views sacrifice as essential in times of acute transition. It can help to assuage the insecurity of a weakened nation confronting more resourceful or progressive neighbors. It is critical to the reconciliation of intergenerational conflict" (195–96). In this respect, she judges *The Awkward Age* to be a privileged novel "because it reveals sacrifice as a preeminent category of thought. It is a text among many because it speaks, in its own rare way, a common language of sacrifice" (197).

While Mizruchi claims for James a certain degree of irony in his portrayal of exclusionary rituals, she nonetheless believes that *acceptance* of scapegoating is the dominant aspect of his work: "James recognized the need for powerful, even brutal forms of cultural repair. Like a missionary confronting a Batta rite, James sees sacrifice as essential to the society of *The Awkward Age*" (249). Thus, while Heyns emphasizes "the subversive and collaborative potential of literary form" (*Expulsion,* 49) in *The Golden Bowl,* Mizruchi characterizes James, in her analysis of *The Awkward Age,* as a writer who acquiesces to the ritual practices that govern his society.

Finally, in *Joseph Conrad and the Art of Sacrifice,* Andrew Mozina—adopting, as did Heyns, a specifically Girardian perspective—characterizes the development of Conrad's oeuvre in terms of its lessening dependence on sacrificial rituals in the construction of its plots. In the course of supporting his thesis, Mozina notes that in *The Nigger of the Narcissus,* the death of James Wait is imbued with primitive sacrificial implications, a fact that leads him to conclude that, "in this early example of Conrad's major phase, we see at work a primitive scapegoat mechanism" (29). In Mozina's view, however, by the time that Conrad reaches the end of his writing career, in such a novel as *Chance,* he has transcended his earlier reliance on this mechanism. In this late novel the violent scapegoating that one finds in *The Nigger of the Narcissus* is replaced by the profession of love involved in the marital reconciliation between Flora and Anthony (134). Mozina concludes from his analyses of these novels, as well as of such intermediary examples as *Lord Jim* and *Under Western Eyes,* that "Conrad's transition from a traditional view of scapegoating to a Christian view of scapegoating was a tumultuous and complex process which produced his best work" (136).

All of these discussions of the novelistic representation of sacrificial rituals underline the presence of an ambivalent attitude toward the practice of scapegoating. The authors of these novels are seen as struggling to divest themselves of an atavistic inheritance whose hold on them proves to be remarkably tenacious. In the modernist novels that I analyze, this ambivalence leads oftentimes to a form of psychic splitting that prevents antithetical attitudes toward scapegoating from confronting each other directly. On the one hand, we have narrators who unequivocally denounce the violence directed against the victims that they have chosen to defend. At the same time, as though they were staging a "return of the repressed," the scapegoating impulses that had been initially rejected are redirected to what may be called, at the risk of some redundancy, a "substitute scapegoat," which they are free to persecute in an equally unequivocal fashion.[11] Thus, the ambivalence that was analyzed, in turn, by Heyns, Mizruchi, and Mozina produces two parallel and virtually autonomous narratives. Since the narrators themselves are oblivious to the contradiction inherent in their attitude, it must be brought to light by their readers.

In *The Turn of the Screw*, for example, the governess, while coming to the defense of Miles, whom she believes to have been unjustly expelled from his boarding school, formulates an accusation against Peter Quint and Miss Jessel that is based on entirely uncorroborated, as well as inconclusive, evidence. Likewise, in *Heart of Darkness*, Marlow, while defending Kurtz against the community that excludes him, does voice his own exclusionary tendencies in his portrayal of black Africans as utterly other than the white European colleagues to whom he is recounting his adventures. The same proclivity is at work in his portrayal of women as fundamentally incapable of contemplating the truth that he willingly reveals to his male listeners. This process of exchanging one excluded figure for another is even more clearly in evidence in *The Good Soldier*, where Dowell, refusing to endorse what he perceives as the communal persecution of Edward, replicates the scapegoating behavior that he attributes to this community in his own denunciation of Leonora and Florence.

The process of substitution involved in scapegoating—whereby an innocent victim is punished in place of a genuinely guilty party—takes an especially ironic turn in *The Great Gatsby*. On the one hand, this process is so blatantly at work in the circumstances leading to the death of Gatsby as a surrogate for Daisy that no reader can fail to observe it. Somewhat less obviously, however, Gatsby also dies as a surrogate for Nick by taking upon himself the burden of the latter's vicarious desires. Furthermore, the "unaffected scorn" that Nick attributes so unpersuasively to his judgment of Gatsby is repeatedly redirected with unfailingly convincing virulence towards such "substitute scapegoats" as Tom and Daisy Buchanan, Meyer Wolfsheim, and, in fact, all of the "friends" who abandon Gatsby after his death. All of these characters must suffer, in the eyes of his assembled readers, the obloquy that Nick is incapable of directing toward himself.

*To the Lighthouse* presents an interesting variation on this process of substitution, in the sense that the redirecting of the sacrificial motive is much more the work of certain of its readers than of its narrator. Readers who interpret this novel sacrificially believe that its narrative movement enacts an exclusionary process whereby Lily Briscoe, who had until now been its unjustly designated victim, is now replaced by Mr. Ramsay, who stands deservedly accused of embodying patriarchal norms. The events of the last section of the novel are sufficiently ambiguous to be interpreted either as representing the restoration of the cultural values embodied by Mr. Ramsay or their wholesale rejection and the implementing of radically new, anti-patriarchal values. Is Mr. Ramsay subjected to a sacrificial expulsion, or does Lily manage to achieve an accommodation with him and the cultural values that he represents? Much recent criticism of the novel has tended, quite unambiguously and without qualification, to opt for the first of these readings.

An intriguing example of this tendency may be noted in Jane Goldman's analysis of the "Time Passes" section of the novel, which she explicitly reads as a modern reworking of an ancient sacrificial ritual. Supporting her argument by references to Woolf's diary entries as well as to her essay on the eclipse of the sun, entitled "The Sun and the Fish," Goldman reads the images of light in this section as representations of patriarchal rationality. The encroaching darkness correspondingly represents the feminine forces that devour or dismember this masculine principle. This sacrificial expulsion of the light then leads to a phase of rejuvenation, marked by what the author describes as the proliferation of "feminist prismatics." Goldman's interpretation uncannily echoes Freud's discussion, in *Totem and Taboo*, of the murder of the patriarchal father by the primal horde as well as Girard's assertion that human communities must direct their destructive violence toward a sacrificial victim in order to create bonds of solidarity among their members. The narrators of

*The Turn of the Screw, Heart of Darkness, The Good Soldier,* and *The Great Gatsby* explicitly invite their readers to direct their moral aggression to the figures that they have selected for exclusion. The narrator of *To the Lighthouse,* for her part, at least hints at such an invitation, to which many readers have willingly responded as though it had been unambiguously offered.

In his well-known article on *Heart of Darkness,* the African novelist Chinua Achebe, having protested against Marlow's distorted image of Africa, claims that his point of view must nevertheless be taken as normative because Conrad himself has failed to provide the reader with "an alternative frame of reference" that is distinct from his narrator's (in Kimbrough, *Heart of Darkness,* 256). In fact, however, each of our novels, including *Heart of Darkness,* does contest its narrator's remystification of scapegoating. They tend, however, to accomplish this goal in less obvious ways than Achebe requires. They do not (with the partial exception of *To the Lighthouse*), resort to morally enlightened narrators, nor do they entrust the process of demystification to the narrative itself (which is, after all, the morally precarious creation of a narrator who is himself susceptible to scapegoating tendencies). Rather, they use the objective pattern of events of the novel, as distinct from the narrator's perspective on them, in such a way as to undermine the sacrificial cause in which he would like to enlist these events.

The sacrificial motive that takes possession of the governess in *The Turn of the Screw* is, for example, implicitly shown to be an expression of her unacknowledged rivalry with the ghosts of her predecessors. In the prologue to his novella, James both acknowledges *and* resolves prospectively the rivalistic impulses that will lead to a tragic outcome in the main story. This frame tale centers on the peaceful competition between Douglas, who is about to tell a ghost story, and his predecessor, a rival storyteller named Griffin. Douglas will triumph over Griffin, not by subjecting him to moral vilification (the strategy adopted by the governess in her response to Peter Quint and Miss Jessel) but by telling a story that—featuring, as it does, a second turn of the screw—will enthrall his audience even more than did Griffin's.

The prosecutorial instinct to which the governess gives expression is also very much in evidence in *The Good Soldier*. In Ford's novel, however, the tempter is merely John Dowell, who, both as a character in the novel and its narrator, is simply too feckless to succeed in imposing the sacrificial schema that he presents as the explanatory pattern of his story. Or so one would hope. In fact, however, as an overview of the novel's critical reception will demonstrate, many readers have been tempted, despite the absence of any plausible evidence in its favor, to accept Dowell's mythic, sacrificial reading. Dowell's mythologizing of his story involves two key distortions: first, his presentation of Edward as an innocent, sacrificial victim who is repeatedly persecuted by society; second, his construction of Leonora and Florence as alternative and, in his view, much deserving scapegoats toward whom he invites his community of readers to direct their unqualified contempt. Many readers of *The Good Soldier* have, in spite of Dowell's patent inadequacies as a reliable guide, found this invitation to relapse into a discredited sacrificial perspective irresistible. Thus, Denis Donoghue interprets the novel as revealing a "neo-Darwinian mutation by which vivid organisms are suppressed so that ordinary, normal, prudent organisms may survive" (Stang, *Presence of Ford Madox Ford*, 52). Likewise, the stigmatizing of Leonora and Florence has generally found a favorable reception, even though the actual events that Dowell recounts do not sustain his scapegoating tactics.

As for *Heart of Darkness*, Achebe had rightly complained that Marlow constructs Africa as a foil for Europe. However, he mistakenly attempts to correct this misapprehension by vaunting the achievements of African civilization, achievements that make it at least the equal of "civilized" Europe. Conrad himself adopts a much profounder strategy for demystifying Marlow's interpretation of his journey. Rather than pointing to an equality of civilized achievements, he draws a parallel between Europe and Africa that is based on the foundational presence—in both the "savage" dark continent and its "civilized" counterpart—of primitive ritual practices. The "unspeakable practices" to which Marlow alludes are thus replicated in the grove of death, where black Africans are left to die beneath the indifferent eyes of their European masters. The worship of Kurtz by the natives is likewise paralleled by the "prayers" that the "pilgrims" whisper to the ivory, which they have elevated to the status of a cult object, as well as by their killing of African natives. Other forms of mythic readings to which Marlow subjects his journey are likewise in evidence. In particular, his elevation of Kurtz—in whose final words he sees unarguable signs of a singular moral victory—is the consequence of an atavistic tendency that is not different in kind from the adoration that the natives direct toward him.

In a similar way, Nick Carraway counts on his readers, who have complied with near unanimity over the decades, to admire Gatsby and to despise the "foul dust"—which is embodied in its most repellant form by Tom and Daisy Buchanan—that arises around him. However, the novel itself repeatedly undercuts the mythic foundation that Nick would construct for it. Gatsby—whose "romantic readiness" Nick vaunts—turns out, in reality, to be as "plagiaristic" as the college acquaintances whose merely imitative desires Nick censures in the opening pages of his narrative. Every detail of Gatsby's behavior—including his affected manner of speech and dress, the heroic wartime feats that he invents for himself, and his wholly predictable pursuit of the young woman who just happened to be pursued by every other young officer stationed in Louisville—all attest to the pervasively borrowed quality of his dream. While Nick is intent upon affirming Gatsby's uniqueness, the facts of his story continually point in the opposite direction—to a Gatsby who has modeled his behavior on the tastes of his social betters and whose lavish parties hint at a longing to be seen in the public eye that renders him barely distinguishable from the other major characters of the novel.

So also the sequence of events in the novel suggests that the responsibility for Gatsby's death, which Nick imputes exclusively to Tom and Daisy, could as legitimately be attributed to himself. Nick chooses not a reveal to Tom the true circumstances of Myrtle Wilson's death; in a deeper way, however, he conceals from himself the fact that the real key to the plot of his story, as well as its ultimate significance, lies in the way in which he has sought throughout the novel to gain covert satisfaction of desires, in particular, the desire to possess what he calls a "romantic woman" (61) and to gain a victory over an envied and redoubtable male rival in the person of Tom Buchanan.

To the Lighthouse likewise presents a narrator who combines a laudable desire to support the cause of an underdog and who at the same

time produces a narrative that, in its turn, encourages a mythic reading that is nevertheless strongly at odds with the demystifying implications of the text itself. Lily Briscoe benefits from the narrator's
solicitude in a way that recalls Marlow's defense of Kurtz and Nick's
of Gatsby. Significantly, however, this narrator does not make extravagant claims on behalf of Lily. There is nothing in *To the Lighthouse*
that equals Nick's inflated claim about Gatsby's "romantic readiness"
or Marlow's certainty as to the "triumph" expressed by Kurtz's dying
words. She has, indeed, defied Mrs. Ramsay's insistence that she
marry, and does, in the novel's concluding pages, complete her
painting. This does not, however, lead to her apotheosis.

In one crucial respect, however, the narrator does, replicating in
this way the attitude of Marlow and Nick, confer upon Lily the mantle of uniqueness and originality that she bears no more convincingly than do Kurtz or Gatsby. By insisting upon Lily's estrangement
from an artistic community whose norms she does not share, the
narrator leads the reader to believe that the completing of the painting is an entirely individual achievement, to which the paintings produced by Lily's fellow painters made no contribution. This mythic
interpretation of Lily's achievement is, however, fundamentally at
odds with the fact that Lily's painting owes as much to impressionism
and post- impressionism as it does to Lily's individual genius. While
the narrator does not specifically allude to the painters or art critics
who have nurtured Lily's creative vision, her description of the style
of Lily's painting leaves no doubt as to its affiliations with the most
innovative work of early-twentieth-century painters. The suppression
of names like Monet, Cézanne, or Woolf's close friend, the art critic
Roger Fry, creates an opportunity to claim for Lily's painting the attributes of a wholly original as well as fundamentally anti-patriarchal
creation. Following this lead, certain readers of the novel have, as I
suggested earlier, adopted a sacrificial reading, whereby the exclusion of Mr. Ramsay, as well as of the cultural accomplishments that
he epitomizes, rather than their assimilation, becomes the ritual act
that brings forth Lily's own artistic achievement.

The novel itself, however, presents Mr. Ramsay in a light that contests the mythic interpretations that would make of him a substitute
scapegoat. His daughter Cam, for example, in spite of deeply hostile
feelings toward her father, remembers him with unmistakable ten-
derness. Woolf herself clearly implies that he is the "unsurpassable

horizon" of productive cultural activity; even his fiercest adversaries in the novel render him this tribute. Thus, James Ramsay, who in the opening pages of the novel is shown hating his father to the point of wishing to kill him, nevertheless instinctively grants that he is the one role model most worthy of emulation, as Woolf herself implicitly reminds us in describing him in terms—"he appeared the image of stark and uncompromising severity" (4)—that unfailingly evoke the image of his father. Also, Lily Briscoe, in whom he provokes feelings of rage at the beginning of "The Lighthouse" section, implicitly acknowledges that he is the one arbiter whose favorable judgment she seeks.

Girard tends to attribute responsibility for misreadings to the reader, who—in spite of the revelation of the truth to which the great novelists invite him—insists on applying "to the work the [erroneous] meanings he already applies to the world" (*Deceit*, 16). At the opposite extreme, we have Achebe's virtual exoneration of readers of *Heart of Darkness*, who have been misled by an author who knowingly chose a subject that was guaranteed to overcome their natural resistance to the "forms of trickery" that he purveys in his novel (in Kimbrough, *Heart of Darkness*, 253). The authors of our novels may, however, be more usefully understood as applying the authorial strategy that Stanley Fish attributes to John Milton in *Surprised by Sin*. Like Fish's Milton, our authors, largely through the narrative voice of their works, lure their readers into making "fallen," atavistic interpretations of events. At the same time, however, they create, through the underlying structure of these same events, an implicit, demystifying countertext that will be available to readers who have successfully resisted the narrator's sacrificial misreadings.

# 1

## Occulted Rivalry in
## *The Turn of the Screw*

In HIS ESSAY ON *THE TURN OF THE SCREW*, WAYNE BOOTH OBSERVES that the plethora of contradictory interpretations that Henry James's novella has inspired leads readers to think of it "as a maze with many intentionally deceptive false turns and dead ends" (Beidler, *Turn of the Screw*, 173). James's readers, in spite of their divergences, are nearly unanimous, however, in assuming that the disturbing events that occur at Bly are to be attributed to the perverse motivations of a designated individual. The governess leads the way along this path by accusing Peter Quint and Miss Jessel of having returned to Bly for malign purposes involving the sexual corruption of the children. The most famous of her followers has been Edmund Wilson who, replicating her belief in some obscure sexual malfeasance as the key to events at Bly, turned the spotlight on the governess herself with his "discovery" that the real culprit is her own unacknowledged sexual frustration.

Most readers of *The Turn of the Screw* echo Wilson by assuming that "hidden" motivations, especially those of a sexual nature, are the most promising place to look for solutions to the riddle posed by James's tale. As I hope to demonstrate in the following pages, however, it is possible to offer a persuasive interpretation of the novella that, although based on simple and uncontroversial facts, leads us to conclusions that are at least as complex and intriguing as readings that take its ostensibly more promising enigmas as their point of departure. All readers, despite their differences with respect to other issues, will agree, for example, that Miss Jessel and Peter Quint *pre-*

*ceded* the governess at Bly and that the governess *accuses* the former
of being a "horror of horrors" (183) and the latter of being "a living
detestable presence" (195). Likewise, no reader will deny that the
governess would like to have a personally satisfying relationship with
the children. Nor is there any disputing the fact that she left behind
a manuscript in which she recounts her version of events and that it
is from this manuscript that Douglas reads on the evening that forms
the setting of the frame tale. Such apparently banal and trivial fac-
tual details are generally scanted in interpretations of the novella in
favor of more ambiguous elements. They may, however, point our attention away from merely distracting enigmas (which may prove to
have been so many red herrings) that James has placed in his novella
and toward the genuine, and genuinely troubling, enigma that is to
be found in our own behavior as readers. The solution to James's riddle may, in other words, reside, not in the moral iniquity of the
ghosts or in the sexual frustration of the governess, but in our own
readiness to serve as compliant witnesses to the unsubstantiated accusation of a malign intent that she brings against the ghosts.

To return for a moment to Wayne Booth's allusion to the "maze"
that James has constructed in *The Turn of the Screw*, we should remember that, for all of the bewilderment that it provokes in one who
is trapped within it, a maze lends itself in the final analysis to one—
and only one—correct solution. Once we have found the only possible way out of a maze, we recognize that the alternative paths were,
quite simply, wrong. We do not ask ourselves why we made a wrong
turn at a particular point; we simply had no way of knowing that we
were in error. As we reflect on James's novella, however, we recognize
that our own willing complicity played an important role in our having followed its false leads. In particular, our readiness to pursue
hints of covert sexual misbehavior led us to overlook the entirely un-
hidden significance of the governess's *belatedness* with respect to the
ghosts and the unacknowledged rivalry that this generates.

Shortly after James published *The Turn of the Screw*, Joseph Conrad—in *Heart of Darkness*, a novel that reverberates with revelations
regarding the European plunder of the African continent—would
play upon our instinctive readiness to accept without question the
idea that cannibalism was the ne plus ultra in the annals of "horror."
Similarly, James shows us the ease with which we are inclined to believe, even in the absence of any compelling evidence, accusations

against individuals who have aroused our irrational suspicions. James himself clearly hints at this largely ignored dimension of his work in his preface to the tale, where he tells us that "Peter Quint and Miss Jessel are not 'ghosts' at all, as we know the ghost, but goblins, elves, imps, demons as loosely constructed as those of the old trials for witchcraft" (41). This evocation of "trials of witchcraft" in the midst of a discussion of *The Turn of the Screw*—which may initially strike us as highly incongruous—points, in fact, with remarkable prescience to the underlying ritual or, more precisely, juridical structure of James's tale. If Peter Quint and Miss Jessel are witches, then, logically, the governess is their prosecutor, and we are their jury.

James himself never establishes unequivocally that either Peter Quint or Miss Jessel are, in fact, guilty of the moral turpitude that the narrator attributes to them. The worst thing that Miss Jessel ever does before our very eyes is to sit at a writing table that the governess believes (on rather slender evidence when one thinks about it) to be *her own* personal property. Unlike the purely speculative and tendentious charges that the governess brings against Miss Jessel, this action is morally neutral. The former governess is simply doing, albeit in the *present* moment, something that she used to do unobjectionably in the *past*. When the governess refers to Miss Jessel as her "vile predecessor" we should, while readily granting that she qualifies for the second of these designations, look upon the first with great skepticism.

Speculation about the ghosts' covert sexual motivations, as well as those of the governess, tends to obscure the more easily verified role played by *rivalry* in her relationships with other characters. She tells us quite revealingly, for example, that potential competition between herself and Mrs. Grose was a subject that greatly concerned her before she arrived at Bly. It is reasonable to infer that the rivalry that she expected to experience with Mrs. Grose, but which failed to materialize, is then reawakened by her encounter with the ghost of Miss Jessel. We should notice, however, that *overt* rivalry is eclipsed by the assumption of moral superiority in this second relationship. In place of a newcomer faced with the morally neutral obligation of having to prove her worth in the shadow of a successful predecessor, we find a young woman who brings *moral accusations* against this predecessor that are so vehement, and so single-minded in their refusal to entertain alternative explanations of her "facts," that she reminds us of nothing so much as a public prosecutor who is intent upon gaining a conviction.[1]

The most powerful critique of the governess in her role as prosecutor was offered by Leon Edel, who argued that "*The Turn of the Screw* is a powerful tale of 'possession,' as in the old fables of demons and dybbuks; and it is the governess who is possessed. . . . In seeking to cope with her own demons she infects those around her—as Hitler, raving and ranting, infected an entire nation with his hysteria" (in Esch and Warren, *Turn of the Screw*, 192). Edel's allusion to Hitler, especially in light of James's remark about "trials of witchcraft," alerts us to the possibility that the place to look for evil in this tale is neither in sexual license nor in frustration, but in the complicitous relationship between rhetorically effective demagogues and their audiences. As was true with Hitler's scapegoating of the Jews, the governess's condemnation of Peter Quint and Miss Jessel converts what was at first merely a *rival* people into *moral* pariahs. Her transformation of the ghosts into scapegoats, which is not based upon observable aspects of their behavior, is produced by her need to validate her claim to superiority: since neither chronology nor social class favors "the youngest of several daughters of a poor country parson" (149) she appeals, instead, to morality as well as to the reliably persecutory tendencies of her implied readers.

The governess's situation in the main story uncannily resembles that of Douglas in the frametale in the sense that both experience anxieties related to their status as "latecomers." The governess had been preceded at Bly by Miss Jessel and Peter Quint. Douglas, on the evening of storytelling which the frame tale takes as its setting, has been preceded by a guest named Griffin (whose story about a ghostly apparition to a young child had held his listeners "round the fire, sufficiently breathless") as well as by an unnamed guest whose story had been judged "not particularly effective" (145). Both Douglas and the governess are thus placed in a similar situation, one that may be expected to arouse feelings of rivalry as well as fears of unworthiness.[2] In elaborating this parallel, James artfully confronts the rivalistic implications of Douglas's predicament directly while diverting attention away from it when presenting the governess. The governess's description of the paradisiacal nature of Bly as she first encounters it leads us to think of this country house as a place from which evil has seemingly been banished. It may, however, be more

accurate to say that Bly is a place where the governess appears to
have no rivals. Thus, she may, immediately upon her arrival there,
think of Flora as "my little girl" (153) without anyone challenging
her right to such a claim. Nor will the children rebuff her because
they miss her predecessors (including not only Miss Jessel and Peter
Quint, but also their grandparents and their father, or perhaps that
most absolute of ghosts, their *mother*, who is never once mentioned
either in the frame tale or in the main story). James has, in his description of the governess's first days at Bly, completely suppressed
every single event that we could plausibly imagine as disturbing her
equanimity.

The fact that the governess is nonetheless susceptible to feelings
of rivalry is clearly established from the moment of her arrival at Bly.
She worries that Mrs. Grose, who undeniably arrived there before
she did, will challenge the obviously gratifying impression, provoked
by the radiant reception that she receives from Flora, that she was
"the mistress or a distinguished visitor" (152). She had already
"rather brooded" about the possibly troubling aspect of her prospec-
tive relationship with Mrs. Grose before arriving at Bly (153). As it
turns out, however, her potential vulnerability as a latecomer to Bly
is resolved from the moment of her arrival by a remarkably (and,
perhaps, implausibly) compliant Mrs. Grose, who has already arranged for a smooth transition from the old guardian to the new.
James further mitigates the potentially troubling consequences of
the governess's belatedness by making Mrs. Grose illiterate, a fact
that the governess discovers upon asking the older woman to read
the letter sent by the headmaster from Miles's school. Mrs. Grose's
inability to read confers upon the governess an unmistakable sign of
social superiority that, in effect, compensates for her chronological
handicap. We may also note that James, by bestowing on the governess an elegant prose style that uncannily resembles his own, considerably augments the advantage that her possession of the gift of
literacy already implies.

Douglas, for his part, has at his disposal comparable means that
allow him to compensate for the unalterable fact that Griffin was
there before him as an audience-pleasing raconteur. It is revelatory,
in this connection, that there was no prototype for Griffin in the
original story upon which James based his novella. As James explains
in his preface, his host on this occasion was motivated not by rivalry

but by altruistic motives. His guests had been lamenting the fact that both the supply and the quality of ghost stories had been subjected to a "marked and sad drop." He hoped, in telling the story that James would later transform into *The Turn of the Screw,* to "have recovered for us one of the scantest of fragments of this form at its very best" (36).

The situation in the frame tale of *The Turn of the Screw* is, to be sure, very different. There, the guests have "been held breathless" by Griffin's magisterial demonstration of the continued vitality of the genre. Douglas, in his turn, is clearly motivated, not by altruistic considerations, but, rather, by the game of one-upmanship that he is playing with Griffin. James underlines Griffin's role as a model whom Douglas would like not only to emulate but to surpass by having the unnamed narrator tell us that Douglas's contribution to the evening's storytelling is immediately provoked by another guest's speculation that Griffin's story must be the only one of its kind. Douglas refutes this claim by asserting, not merely that he knows another story of the same type, but—in a move that points to anxieties about belatedness that align him with the governess—that Griffin's story is "not the *first* occurrence of its charming kind" (145; my emphasis). How Douglas happens to know that his story precedes Griffin's (or even what, precisely, such a claim means) is left unclear. Having made an unprovable claim on behalf of his story (one that disputes not simply the *uniqueness* but, more tellingly, the *priority* of Griffin's story), Douglas then asserts, more plausibly, that it is a better story because it contains two ghosts rather than just one. In a self-promoting gesture for which there is no prototype in the original circumstances of James's hearing this story, Douglas claims that "Nobody but me, till now, has ever heard" this tale. The unnamed narrator, in his turn, emphasizes the competitive stakes when he says of Douglas that he "with quiet art, prepared his triumph" (9–10).

The invention of Griffin, and the symmetrical relationship that this creates between Douglas and the governess as characters who must compensate for their predicament as latecomers, provides crucial insight into the nature of the quandary in which James places the governess. Douglas is not, however, merely a later version of the governess who must, in his turn, experience anxieties provoked by the recognition of his belatedness. Rather, he is the medium through which James explores the possibility of resolving in a peaceful way a dilemma that produces, in the main story, an entirely tragic outcome. Having successfully dealt with the threat to her priority posed by Mrs. Grose, the governess will founder, with tragic consequences, on the more obdurate threat represented by Peter Quint and Miss Jessel. Douglas—and, by implication James himself—by frankly acknowledging his dependence on his predecessors (in particular, the governess) will escape the rivalistic impasse to which his initial instinct to compete with Griffin may otherwise have led him.

Along with Griffin—a marginal figure who nonetheless contributes significantly to the symmetry that binds the frame tale to the main story, James also added to the germ of *The Turn of the Screw* the detail of the manuscript that Douglas inherited from the governess and that he will, shortly before his own death, bequeath to the unnamed narrator. This seemingly insignificant detail serves to underline Douglas's indebtedness to the governess for the story with which he will regale his audience, an indebtedness that does not significantly diminish his confident expectation that the eventual performance will be *his* "triumph." The notable lack of any "anxiety of influence" in Douglas's relationship with his precursor contrasts significantly with the governess's fundamentally adversarial attitude toward the ghostly predecessors that disturb her equanimity at Bly.[3] In this way, it provides, already in the prologue, the resolution to the central conflict of the main story, which James's original readers expected to find in an epilogue.

The governess returns to James's tale, not in her own person (as had Peter Quint and Miss Jessel) but, rather, in the form of a manuscript that serves for Douglas, not as an unwanted intrusion that thwarts his aspiration to preeminence, but as a creative occasion that will enhance his prestige in the eyes of his audience. The arrival of the manuscript, and the ghost story that it relates, is, in a process that completely reverses the situation found in the main story, positively desired, not only by the audience, but by Douglas himself. His own expectation that the manuscript will contribute to his "triumph" is a reversed mirroring of the governess's less clearly avowed fear of being defeated by the ghosts. The governess thinks of her performance at Bly as a *moral* victory (akin to Douglas's *artistic* triumph); it is, however, one that is achieved at the expense of, rather than thanks to, her predecessors.

Mirroring Douglas, James freely and openly acknowledges the priority of his precursors. In the preface he praises the Brothers Grimm for having perfected the compact form of the fairy tale, while pointing to the *Arabian Nights* as the most highly elaborated example of the loosely organized, rambling form of this genre. Within the main story itself, he alludes directly to his immediate precursors among British novelists when he has the governess, after seeing Peter Quint for the first time, ask herself: "Was there a 'secret' at Bly—a mystery of Udolpho or an insane, an unmentionable relative kept in unsuspected confinement?" (166). The first of these surmises directly alludes to the celebrated novel by Ann Radcliffe, while the second points to the "mad woman in the attic" motif found in Charlotte Brontë's *Jane Eyre*.

In a somewhat less obvious way, James draws upon the popular literary genre of the "governess novel" as well as of novels that feature children as principal characters. Critics of *The Turn of the Screw* have amply documented James's borrowings from his various precursor texts.[4] We should notice, along with the details themselves, the equally important fact that James himself consciously foregrounds these borrowings, knowing perfectly well that our recognizing their cumulative presence in his novella will not in the least detract from our admiration for his own individual achievement. We may be pertinently reminded here of Mrs. Grose's admonition to the governess, in which she reminds her that numerous young women have attracted the uncle's attention: "Well, Miss, you're not the first—and you won't be the last" (154). The governess's less-than-candid reply to this warning ("Oh I've no pretensions . . . to being the only one") acknowledges, albeit in a statement that has been distorted by her resort to hypocritical negation (as well as by a telling shift of emphasis from *priority* to *uniqueness*), her susceptibility to the universal human longing to be "more equal" than anyone else. How, *The Turn of the Screw* implicitly asks, can we resolve the conflict between our inextinguishable desire for priority and our inevitable relegation to the position of latecomers?

Douglas's solution is immediate and unproblematic. He will bring to life in the form of an *oral* performance a *written* text; the strict division of labor between the oral and the written that underlies his performance rules out any possibility of competition. He does not have to "one up" the governess in order that his perfor-

mance be regarded as a triumph. From the initial reaction of his audience—"Oh how delicious!" (146)—we may deduce that the governess has given him precisely the story that will assure his success.
The perennial appeal of *The Turn of the Screw* likewise indicates that
James's creative transformation of his sources has created a work of
lasting, as well as of individual, distinction.

Both Douglas and the governess (at least initially) deal effectively
with anxieties regarding their belatedness. Douglas has in his keeping an unbeatable ghost story, and the governess, in a neat mirroring
of this fortunate circumstance, possesses the gift of literacy as well as
a compliant predecessor in the person of Mrs. Grose. The arrival of
the ghosts, however, reawakens her initial anxieties in a way that allows of no peaceful, cooperative resolution. The far more imposing
challenge that they provoke should not, however, lead us to overlook
the fundamental similarity that makes of the bulk of the main story a
disguised repetition of the situation in which the governess found
herself upon her arrival at Bly, a situation that Douglas will confront
years later at the home of his host. In all three episodes, a desired
bond with another person or a group of people is potentially
threatened by the presence of a third party (respectively, Mrs.
Grose, the ghosts, and Griffin). Our recognizing this symmetry—
despite James's having obscured it by placing one episode in the
frame tale, another in an essentially realistic account of the governess's first meeting with Mrs. Grose, and yet another in a ghost
story—prepares us to see that the conflict that failed to materialize
in the frame tale and in the first pages of the governess's narrative in
the first two episodes, returns with an overwhelming force with the
arrival of the ghosts.

The governess herself recounts the "ghostly" part of her narrative
in such a way as to lead us to believe that she is fundamentally *different* from Peter Quint and Miss Jessel. They, to begin with, are ghosts
of the dead, while she is a living human being. To this distinction,
she adds a crucial *moral* difference: she is a fundamentally good protagonist who is called upon by her present circumstances to do bat-
tle with antagonists who are irredeemably corrupt. Even critics who
question the reliability of the governess's narrative tend to assume
that "evil" may be unproblematically attributed to ghosts. James himself, however, reminds us that ghosts are not inherently evil in his
notebook entry entitled "Subject for a Ghost-Story." There, he

sketches a story in which a protagonist who suffers from "some great and constant trouble" is visited by a spirit who comes in the hope "that it might interpose, redeem and protect" (in Esch and Warren, *Turn of the Screw*, 100).

It may be more reasonable to assume that evil, such as it exists in *The Turn of the Screw*, is not essentially a moral defect that inheres objectively in an *individual* character (whether a ghostly libertine or a living, yet frustrated spinster). Rather, it is a *relational* quality that spontaneously, and fatally, marks the encounter between a successful predecessor and a belated aspirant. James, with his own "quiet art," presents this encounter much more overtly at the margins (that is, in the frame tale and in the governess's first meeting with Mrs. Grose) of *The Turn of the Screw* than in its major episode. Wherever it appears in the novella, it involves the experience of encountering someone who is essentially like oneself and who may possess the stronger claim to the place that one would like to occupy. Despite her insistence on the fundamental moral differences that distinguish her from the ghosts, the governess, whose very title points to her "hybrid" social status, is every bit as much of an intruder at Bly as are her ghostly counterparts. In this respect, Millicent Bell has some very pertinent remarks on the ambiguity inherent in the role of governess (in Ian Bell, *Henry James*, 93–94), and David McWhirter has spoken of the "oxymoronic conjunction of 'woman' and 'authority'" that is implied by the title whereby James designates her (in Pollak, *New Essays*, 130).

The fact that Peter Quint and Miss Jessel preceded the governess at Bly is not in itself a morally charged issue. Morality, rather, is the weapon that she chooses—just as Douglas will, in his turn, resort to "quiet art"—to assert her own priority in a situation in which the facts of chronology do not favor her claim. Her rejoinder to Mrs. Grose's comment about many young women having caught the master's eye—"'Oh I've not pretensions,' I could laugh, 'to being the only one'" (154) uses the language of denial to suggest the unavowed longing for priority that identifies her with Douglas and helps us trace her narrative back to its origin in a perceived, if not quite acknowledged, disadvantage in her relationship with the ghosts. The only evidence in support of the moral accusation that the governess brings against the ghosts comes from unconfirmed statements made by Mrs. Grose. Even if we accept as true her claim that the former servants were guilty of a sexual dereliction, this does not necessarily justify the conclusion that they have returned to Bly with some malign intent. This is purely an inference based on some vague, unconfirmed clues concerning their presumed waywardness when they were alive.[5] The readiness of the novella's readers to accept with quasi-unanimity the veracity of Mrs. Grose's statements alerts us to the possibility that its deeper ethical interest may rest with the way that—while seeming to direct our attention to the psychology of a designated *individual*—it actually explores our own psychology as a *community* of readers.

All that we know beyond any doubt is that the governess believes that Miss Jessel and Peter Quint enjoyed a relationship with "her" children whose intensity was such that it has survived their physical deaths. The predicament in which she finds herself replicates her relationship with the uncle. In both cases, desire for human contact and recognition is inseparable from an obstacle that prevents its fulfillment. She cannot contact the uncle without sacrificing the "heroic" conduct that she would like him to admire in her; likewise, she cannot desire friendship with the children without imagining that this has been made impossible by her predecessors. We may conclude from this that the key to our understanding her behavior is not repressed erotic desire so much as it is her susceptibility to situations that create for her a double-bind. So susceptible is she, in fact, that she will invent these situations when they fail to occur in reality. The uncle's order that she not communicate with him is real. Her desire for friendship with the children is not, however, impeded by an actual obstacle; Mrs. Grose, her only potential rival, is, as we have already seen, remarkably compliant.

Thus, the arrival of the ghosts will, in effect, create precisely that obstacle that had failed to appear upon her own arrival at Bly. For this reason, her specific relationships—whether with the uncle, or with Mrs. Grose or with the children—should not be thought of as the originating circumstances whose psychological consequences are echoed throughout her narrative. It is neither to her erotic yearning for the uncle, nor to the inherent evil (whether of the children or the ghosts) that we must look for clues to the mystery of the novella. No one of these relationships is, properly speaking, originary. Rather, each one of them exemplifies, in no particular order of precedence, the truly originary, and implacable rule whereby the onset of a desire must necessarily be accompanied by some factor that will guarantee its frustration.

Rather than allowing ourselves to be unnecessarily distracted by the false issue of the ghosts as real or as projections, we may with much greater pertinence ask ourselves what would have been the outcome if the ghosts that returned to Bly had not been those of Miss Jessel and Peter Quint, but other adults from the children's past that they could equally well be imagined as missing. James could, for example, have arranged the return in ghostly form of the children's parents, or of their doubtlessly beloved grandparents, for that matter. We recognize intuitively that this eventuality would have presented the governess with an even greater quandary than the one that she does have to face. On what grounds, if *these* ghosts returned, could she possibly claim her own priority? In this respect, the most telling detail regarding the covert strategy at work in the governess's narrative may not be her preoccupation with the ghosts, but her absolute avoidance (amounting to a symptomatic refusal) of any thoughts about the deceased members of the children's family. The return of Peter Quint and Miss Jessel may thus be interpreted as a protective screen that spares the governess's having to face genuinely insurmountable proof of her irreversible belatedness.

The governess reveals her longing for priority—her desire to bestow upon herself the emblems of uncontestable preeminence—throughout her narrative. Thus, she pictures herself in the early phase of her stay at Bly, not merely as a lowly governess but, rather grandiloquently, as the captain of "a great drifting ship" (156) whose passengers are, by implication, uniquely dependent on her for their own well-being. Later, after discovering that Miles has been expelled from school—and even before encountering Quint's ghost for the first time—she imagines herself as "a remarkable young woman" who "took comfort in the faith that this would more publicly appear." She then confides to us, in an artful piece of foreshadowing, that she "needed to be remarkable to offer a front to the remarkable things that presently gave their first signs" (163).

The cause-effect relationship implied by this assertion should, however, give us pause. We may, in other words, reasonably ask ourselves whether, as the governess assumes, a reputation for remarkableness will be the consequence of the events or whether the "events" themselves are the consequence of her desire to be seen as remarkable. As we have just noticed, James could easily have produced alternative ghostly apparitions that would not have had such a self-enhancing outcome. Even such ghosts as do appear do not inherently lend themselves to the public confirmation of her heroic qualities that the governess desires; in order that they serve her purposes, they must be refashioned as hostile, demonic figures who endanger the little community whose well-being has been entrusted to her.[6]

For Edmund Wilson, the illicit sexual behavior that the governess, with some coaching from Mrs. Grose, attributes to Peter Quint and Miss Jessel is to be read as a projection of her own thwarted sexual longings. It may, however, be more accurate to read her accusation of morally objectionable behavior as a "window of opportunity" for a young woman—"the youngest of several daughters of a poor country parson" (149)—who is intent upon demonstrating her superiority in the midst of objectively unpromising circumstances. As I suggested earlier, the *moral* corruption that she attributes to the ghosts creates for her the possibility of an eventual victory comparable to the triumph that Douglas will gain over Griffith, whose own story is marked by the *aesthetic* defect of its having only one ghost.

As part of the unconscious strategy that she adopts in the pursuit of her own triumph, the governess will repeatedly stress the great differences that distinguish her from the ghosts. As some readers have noted, however, obvious similarities create an indisputable—though, at the same time, an unacknowledged—bond between the three. In this respect, we could argue that the "repression" that lies at the heart of *The Turn of the Screw* concerns, not sexual desire, but the recognition of similarities between oneself and a potential, or actual, rival. The governess's narrative is replete with details that alert us to the resemblances that make of her, whether she recognizes this or not, a mirror image of her antagonists. Like them, she is an interloper at Bly who entertains fantasies regarding her possible social advancement. Miss Jessel may have hoped to attract the attention of the uncle; Peter Quint did find vicarious satisfaction in wearing his clothes. The governess herself, while not entering the upper class through the marriage to the uncle that she doubtlessly desired will indirectly satisfy her yearnings by "wearing" the prose style of Henry James in the form of a narrative that will find great favor amidst a cultivated and highly literate audience.

As other readers have noted, the hybrid, transgressive quality denoted by the word "ghost" is replicated in the title "governess" by which the young woman, in the absence of a proper name, is designated throughout *The Turn of the Screw.* Just as the ghosts are poised ambiguously, and uncannily, between the realms of the living and of the dead, the governess is suspended between two social classes, as well as between two genders. She bears a title whose opening syllables resonate with the promise of male privilege, but which concludes with a suffix that consigns her to a subaltern position. It is a title that evokes, as well, a social class decidedly different from the one that she knew as the daughter of a "poor country parson."

Bruce Robbins has offered a fascinating analysis of the interplay of sameness and difference as it applies to the relationship between the governess and the ghosts. He begins by noting that *The Turn of the Screw* "systematically confuses ghosts with servants—both categories impalpable, alien and threatening" (in Esch and Warren, *Turn of the Screw,* 238). Robbins relates this feature of the novella to Frederic Jameson's observation that "romance gives a symbolic answer to the question: how can my enemy be thought as *evil* (marked by some absolute difference from myself) when his conduct is *identical* to mine." In classic examples of romance this conflict is resolved by a final scene in which the "hostile knight reveals his identity, thus losing his sinister unfamiliarity." For Robbins, the clue to our understanding of *The Turn of the Screw* is to be found in the realization that it, on the contrary, contains no culminating scene in which the antagonist ceases to be a villain in the eyes of the protagonist. As Robbins notes, in the absence of such a scene "parallels, mirroring relationship among scenes, can be interpreted as continual, unanswered beckonings to a recognition that would convert these threatening aliens into mere visions of herself" (in Esch and Warren, *Turn of the Screw,* 239). This observation leads him to conclude that *The Turn of the Screw* projects, without actually achieving, a "happy end" characterized by "the return to Bly to the (classless) Edenic state in which the governess first found it, the evaporation from her world of the 'evil' that she added to it, which would result from her recognition of what so many voices are trying to tell her—her identity with the others" (240).

In spite of the astuteness of many details of his analysis, however, Robbins's conclusion is patently naïve in its assumption that the governess's recognition of the identity between herself and the ghosts would have produced a happy ending to the novella. On the contrary, as René Girard has argued, and as ordinary experience never ceases to confirm, the discovery that other people want the same things that we want is more likely to produce conflict than harmony. From a certain perspective, the governess understands perfectly well her similarity to Peter Quint and Miss Jessel. Both she and the ghosts want the same thing: friendship with, or recognition from, Miles and Flora. Each faces a comparable obstacle, which inhibits fulfillment of this desire: an abyss exists between the ghosts of Peter Quint and Miss Jessel and the world of the living; the governess must, in her turn, deal with such equally unbreachable barriers as the impossibility of contacting the uncle and her nearly invincible reluctance to confront Miles and Flora directly. In a deeper way, she must confront a liability that is almost as intractable as death itself: she is the latecomer who must live in the shadow, if not of death itself, then at least of her predecessors.

Signs of the underlying identity between the governess and the ghosts abound in the novella. She is prevented from recognizing them, however, by her unformulated, yet clearly implied, recognition that she would lose her claim "to being the only one" if she were to admit to herself how much she shared in common with her presumed antagonists. In this respect, one of the most revelatory episodes in *The Turn of the Screw* occurs when the governess enters the schoolroom only to discover that Miss Jessel, having preceded her in more ways than one, has laid a perceptibly unnerving claim to the writing table: "Seated at my own table in the clear noonday light I saw a person whom, without my previous experience, I should have taken at the first blush for some housemaid who might have stayed at home to look after the place and who, availing herself of rare relief from observation and of the schoolroom table and my pens, ink and paper, had applied herself to the considerable effort of a letter to her sweetheart" (221).

Accepting the logic of Robbins's argument would lead us to expect the governess—upon seeing so clearly in Miss Jessel's situation a mirror image of her own—to welcome her with open arms to Bly. James, however, in a move that proves him to be the better psychologist, shows the governess as responding in an obviously panicky way. Of paramount interest is the fact that she does not simply react to Miss Jessel as though the latter were a mere intruder. Instead, in a moment of heightened lucidity, she recognizes that she and Miss Jessel are interchangeable. Rather than seeing in this resemblance the possibility of their friendship, however, she responds intuitively to its lethal implications: "she had looked at me long enough to appear to say that her right to sit at my table was as good as mine to sit at hers. While these instants lasted indeed I had the extraordinary chill of a feeling that it was I who was the intruder" (221).

This is precisely the scene of reciprocal identification that Robbins does not find in *The Turn of the Screw*. Its presence is so easily overlooked because it has none of the harmonious aura predicted for it by the theory that he borrows from Jameson. The governess's designation of Miss Jessel as "my vile predecessor" in this scene points to the violent feelings that her encounter with her own likeness has spontaneously provoked in her. As Ned Lukacher has correctly noted with respect to another episode, "[i]n Jessel's desire to possess the souls of the children, the governess sees her own desire to seize upon the children's unconscious desire" (in Esch and Warren, *Turn of the Screw*, 244). By rising from what the governess has just called (but on whose authority?) *my* table and, by directly approaching her, Miss Jessel intensifies a symmetry that her replacement must necessarily experience as menacing. We may wonder on what evidence the new governess characterizes Miss Jessel as "vile." Even if the former governess had had an illicit sexual relationship with Peter Quint, the word that she chooses is patently disproportionate to its occasion. The justification of her choice is to be found, not in the actual circumstances of Miss Jessel's past, but in the simple, and morally neutral fact, of her being the governess's predecessor. Thus, the expression "my vile predecessor," which may initially strike some readers as a tendentious *hyperbole*, turns out, upon inspection, to be actually a *redundancy*.

In suggesting that *The Turn of the Screw* gestures toward a recognition without ever achieving it, Robbins also overlooks the resolution of rivalistic conflict that does occur, as we have already seen, in the cooperative relationship with the governess that allows Douglas (another latecomer) to practice his one-upmanship on Griffin. It is precisely because Douglas does not try to appropriate the governess's identity—by, for example, claiming to be the author of the story that he is about to narrate—that he is able to relate to her in an entirely unproblematic way. In this respect, his "appropriation" of her manuscript (his proprietorship over which is reinforced by the fact that it is kept in a *locked* drawer to which he *alone* has the key) signifies the novella's resolution of the otherwise irresolvable conflict over ownership that surfaces in the schoolroom scene between the governess and Miss Jessel.

The manuscript becomes successively the property of various "owners"—each of whose claim to ownership is based on a different functional relationship to it: as author, as copyist, and as performer (to which we could perhaps add our relationship as its readers and interpreters). However, the worktable in the schoolroom—as the governess's simultaneously hyperbolic and redundant epithet indicates—does not lend itself to such freedom of possession. This freefloating quality of the manuscript points to the way that James has already arranged, in the prologue to his tale, the resolution that we look for futilely in the main story. It is, however, a resolution that puts an end to *rivalry* rather than answering questions about the *reliability* of the governess's narrative.

Another example of an element in the novella that lends itself to alternatively harmonious and discordant responses has to do with the ghosts themselves. For reasons that should be clear by now, the governess experiences her own encounter with the ghosts of her predecessors as a catastrophe or, at best, a challenge that will allow her to display her heroic qualities. Once she has learned from Mrs. Grose the incriminating details (proving not so much that the former servants were unutterably evil as that they had enjoyed a privileged relationship with the children) the governess does not miss an opportunity to pillory them before the eyes of her readers.

Ghosts are not, however, inherently evil; nor are they an exclusively troubling presence in *The Turn of the Screw*. In contrast to the horror that the ghostly visitations of Peter Quint and Miss Jessel inspire in the governess, literary evocations of ghosts arouse delight in the guests who are about to be entertained by Douglas's performance. "Oh how delicious!" cries one of the women upon hearing that his story will be unsurpassed for sheer "dreadfulness" (146). And even the ladies, who will eventually leave before the manuscript arrives, would have liked very much to hear it. Nor is the enjoyment of ghostly apparitions limited to the guests. Throughout our reading of *The Turn of the Screw*, we also experience the pleasurable appearances of these ghosts.

Unlike the assembled guests, we are not required to await the arrival of the manuscript and the beginning of the ghost story in order to experience these pleasurable apparitions. We encounter them right from the beginning of the frame tale itself, in which the ghostly Henry James, exercising his own "quiet art," alerts us to the fact that all of the guests who have gathered that evening, and whose responses to the occasion he is rendering in so vivid and "lifelike" a way, are all in fact quite dead and were, at the time of the frame tale, already well on *their* way to becoming ghosts. We should remember, in this respect, that the governess, not having been forewarned that Peter Quint is dead before she encounters his ghost for the first time, believes him to be a living person. We, in our turn, have a similar experience in our response to Douglas, whom we first see as he is preparing his "triumph" over Griffin. We then feel at least moderated intimations of the uncanny when the narrator continues: "Poor Douglas, before his death—when it was in sight—committed to me the manuscript that reached him on the third of these days" (148). Information regarding Douglas's death, which would have seemed perfectly natural if, for example, it were placed in an epilogue, becomes curiously unsettling when placed in a prologue wherein we learn that the Douglas who is about to triumph over Griffin has been long dead and buried. His "ghost" will, as it were, return to us through the words of James's tale.

Likewise, the governess, herself long dead, will, once the prologue itself has ended, speak to the guests through Douglas, whose own personal identity has been uncannily appropriated for the occasion: "But Douglas, without heeding me, had begun to read with a fine clearness that was like a rendering to the ear of the beauty of his author's hand" (151). Surely, a major dimension of *The Turn of the Screw*, especially its uncanny effects, is lost if we lose sight (or hearing) of the fact that the "feminine" eye-witness account of the governess is being mediated for us by the masculine voice of Douglas. Thus, the medium through which her tale is transmitted is as ambiguously hybrid a figure (although in a moderated and reassuringly contained way) to his listeners as are the ghostly Peter Quint and Miss Jessel. "I remember the whole beginning as a succession of flights and drops" (152) begins the narrative of a dead woman—who speaks to us through the voice of an apparently living but actually dead man—to a fictional audience, which, had it ever lived, would have died long before the narrative, later transmitted to the now no longer living unnamed narrator, was read by the novella's audience, which will, in its turn, eventually join the company of its already deceased predecessors.

The rhetorical strategy that James adopts in informing us of Douglas's death—whereby he places this information almost parenthetically in a sentence that otherwise concerns the activities of the living—applies to his portrayal of other characters as well. Thus, we are told of Miss Jessel that "she was a most respectable person—till her death, the great awkwardness of which, had, precisely, left no alternative but the school for little Miles" (150). Similarly, the governess's death is mentioned briefly and subordinately in a sentence whose principal purpose is to explain how Douglas came into possession of her manuscript: "She had been dead these twenty years. . . . She sent me the pages in question before she died" (146). A similar effect may be noted in Douglas's way of introducing the children: "He [their uncle] had been left, by the death of his parents in India, guardian to a small nephew and a small niece, children of a younger, a military brother whom he had lost two years before" (149).

This technique, whereby James leads us to experience the lives of the children as shadowed by the deaths of their grandparents and their father (while curiously overlooking their mother) creates an effect that is as eerie as what the governess must endure at Bly. It is not so much the ghosts of the dead ancestors that we experience at such a moment, but of James himself, who, as the invisible arranger of these repeatedly returning patterns, offers us a coy glimpse of his own otherwise occulted presence. These repetitions induce us to recognize at some point in our reading that the supreme ghost is James himself, who stages his own return, mediated by the various hands through which his text has passed, on every page and, in fact, in every word of *The Turn of the Screw*. As Shoshana Felman has observed, "literature . . . is nothing other than the Master's death, the Master's transformation into a ghost" (in Esch and Warren, *Turn of the Screw*, 227). We may approach as closely as we ever can to the mystery of the novella by contemplating the disparity between the thrill that we experience in sensing James's presence as we read his mediated words and the ever-deepening horror produced in the governess by the ghosts of Peter Quint and Miss Jessel.

We have perhaps already detected signs of James's presence in the strangely coincidental pervasiveness of things that happen twice in his novella. The title itself, as we learn on the first page, refers to a second story that will feature, not only two children, but also the ghosts of two former servants. Likewise, a double sequence of deaths —of parents and (only then) of the grandparents—will set the principal events of the main story in motion. Not only will the governess's story be twice rendered—in her written account and in Douglas's oral performance of this—but also twice transcribed, first by Douglas and then by the unnamed narrator. Finally, as I have already argued, James organizes the frame tale in such a way as to make it a reenactment, albeit this time with a successful outcome, of the encounter with ghosts that the governess experiences in a highly problematic way.

James's presence is also unmistakable, as well as delightfully uncanny, in the mirroring relationship between the first sentence of the frame tale and the last sentence of the main story. The novella begins in the voice of the unnamed narrator: "The story had held us, round the fire, sufficiently breathless" (145) and concludes in the voice of the governess: "I began to feel what it truly was that I held. We were alone with the quiet day, and his little heart, dispossessed, had stopped" (262). The symmetry of the two sentences—whereby the audience that is "held" by a story becomes the corpse of Miles "held" by the governess, and a metaphorical pause in breathing becomes a heart that, quite literally, will never beat again—stages the return of James's own ghost. We may also wonder if the legendary, and much-loved, Jamesian ambiguity alerts us to his ghostly presence when Douglas says, "'I quite agree—in regard to Griffin's ghost, or whatever it was" (145). He means, of course, the ghost that appears in the story narrated by Griffin, but it is difficult for this expression not to remind us of the fact that Griffin himself has, by now, become a ghost.

James's silent, but nonetheless vivid, appearance to his gratefully welcoming readers mirrors the equally—though, in this case, troubling—silence of Peter Quint and Miss Jessel in their successive appearances to the governess. The expectation of a "delicious" experience voiced by one of Douglas's listeners upon learning that his tale will feature two children, will be given to ourselves as readers, not so much by the ghosts who reappear at Bly, as by the Jamesian ghost who returns to the pages of his novella. We should notice in passing (to return briefly to Wilson's interpretation and its aftermath) that the question as to whether James is "really" there in *The Turn of the Screw* or whether we project his presence onto its pages is utterly irrelevant to its emotional truth. The intensity of this impression of a ghostly presence counts significantly more than does its validity or "reliability." The terror that the ghosts provoke in the governess allow her (and, indirectly, ourselves) to experience in a vivid, though uncomprehended, way anxieties about her own belatedness. We, for our part, spontaneously experience the comparable discovery of our own belatedness as readers of the novella rather than its author in a way that provokes only gratitude. If any repressed desire is involved here it is to be found—not in the sexual frustrations of the governess—but in our own longing to be in the presence of a masterful storyteller.

Discussion of *The Turn of the Screw* against the background of James's career in the 1890s has tended to focus on the impact of his failure to achieve popular success as a playwright and, in particular, the trauma of the debacle surrounding his play *Guy Domville*. There is some consensus regarding the new direction that James's career as a novelist took following this failure. He seems, in particular, to have decided to write for an elite audience, one that would appreciate the literary refinements that excited such derision on the part of the London theatergoing public. Thus, David McWhirter suggests that "after the failure of his attempt to achieve popular success with *Guy Domville* (1895) James tried, with his experimental writing, to cultivate a new, more specialized community of readers" (in Pollack, *New Essays*, 123). Something of this ambition may be found in *The Turn of the Screw* (despite James's having dismissed it as a potboiler) especially in Douglas's admonition to his listeners that "[t]he story won't tell . . . not in any literal vulgar way" (147), and in the unnamed narrator's observation that the departure of the ladies has made Douglas's "final auditory more compact and select" (148). We may even detect a residue of *Guy Domville* in the fact that Peter Quint appears to the governess as though he were an "actor" and in her description of Bly in the autumn as being like an empty theater after a performance.

No one to my knowledge, however, has commented on the fact that the frame tale restages James's humiliation at the premiere of

*Guy Domville* in a way that produces a compensatory "triumph." In this respect, it may be worth noting that this is one of the very few of James's fictional works in which the narrative situation is presented in the form of a public performance. This detail, in a work written in the shadow of *Guy Domville,* should encourage us to see in Douglas's assured and unproblematic success with his audience precisely the reaction to his own theatrical performance for which James had hoped. By picturing Douglas as a performer entertaining an audience, James came as close as he ever would in his fictional work to casting his narrator in the role of an *actor.* As though to give even greater concreteness to this underlying metaphor, James invents the otherwise unnecessary (and not particularly Jamesian) detail of the manuscript. The document bequeathed by the governess to Douglas—as a *written* text that will inspire an *oral* performance—neatly approximates the text that the author of a play transmits to his actors. We should notice as well that the division of labor between author and actor in their theatrical undertaking effectively defuses—as it does in the relationship between the governess and Mrs. Grose with respect to the children—the rivalistic discord that may otherwise have prevailed.

In this respect, *The Turn of the Screw,* like *To the Lighthouse,* may be read as a novel that explores the alternatively creative and destructive consequences of crossing boundaries. In Woolf's novel, disrespect for national boundaries produces not only the war alluded to in the "Time Passes" section, but also the Boeuf en Daube which, invented by *French* cooks, is produced for the Ramsays' dinner guests by their *English* cook Mildred. Likewise, the crossing of social boundaries, whether of class or of gender, produces Tansley's fantasy of blowing all these "mild cultivated people" sky high, but also Lily Briscoe's "transgressive" achievement in a cultural realm that had been exclusively coded as male.

So also, James begins his main story with the unobjectionable and, in fact, quite desirable arrival of an outsider to Bly in the form of the new governess. He then precipitates a destructive reenactment of this same action by staging the appearance, not of yet another country parson's daughter, but of the ghosts of Miss Jessel and Peter Quint, whose resemblance to their fellow outsider, while patent, will remain largely invisible to most readers as well as to the governess herself. From this perspective, the proliferation of hybrid figures in *The Turn of the Screw* may be read as a creative restaging of a situation that is lived in a destructive and ultimately tragic way by the governess. Beginning with the hybrid of "Griffin's ghost" (doubly hybrid, in fact, since it is both Griffin himself and the ghost in his story), we move on to Douglas, whose masculine voice replicates the feminine handwriting of the governess, the governess herself (whose title contains a hierarchical ambiguity), Douglas's listeners who are, at once, full of anticipation and long dead, the novella itself, which is formed by the mirroring, ghostly relationship between the frame tale and the main story, and, finally, the ghost of James himself, who appears to us not as a ghost atop a tower or lurking behind a window, but in a plethora of details that we read simultaneously as mere coincidences and as signs of his controlling presence.

*The Turn of the Screw*, which has for obvious reasons been read largely in psychological terms, begs to be read as a persecution narrative whose purpose is to resolve the unrecognized conflict produced in the governess by the reappearance in the form of ghosts of the predecessors whom she had naively expected to supplant in an unproblematic way.[7] This transformation of an unacknowledged personal conflict into a public accusation that has no empirical basis goes, to be sure, entirely unperceived by the governess and by most members of her audience.[8] The governess does, however, point at least indirectly to the ritualistic implications of her situation when she speculates that she has been chosen as an "expiatory victim." We may, in our turn, plausibly imagine that this role is actually played by Miles, who dies of the heart failure that she has induced in him, and, to a lesser extent, by Flora, who succumbs to an illness that requires her departure from Bly.

One of Douglas's listeners in the frame tale asks, upon hearing of Miss Jessel's death, wonders if "necessary danger to life" (150) is an inherent feature of the position of governess itself. In James's novella, to be sure, such dangers as do exist will be repeatedly displaced upon other characters. This scapegoating process is already at work as early as the governess's wholly unfounded "shock of certitude that it was not for me he [the ghost of Peter Quint] had come. He had come for someone else" (169). The governess's seemingly spontaneous and personal intuition replicates the process of displacement upon which the practice of scapegoating has been founded since its inception. The "someone else" to whom she alludes will, in the form of Miles, play throughout the main story the role of expiatory victim that she will disingenuously attribute to herself.[9] A similar process is clearly at work when, having been shocked by her encounter with Peter Quint, she gives to Mrs. Grose "something of the shock that I had received" (170) by gazing at her, in turn, through the window.

James himself, as I noted in the introduction, lends credence to this interpretation in his preface, in which he associates the ghosts of Peter Quint and Miss Jessel with "the old trials for witchcraft" (41). It is worth noting here, not only that James alludes specifically to ritual persecution in his mention of "witchcraft," but also that the string of synonyms that he adduces in particularizing his ghosts all convey the aura of popular, or collective, superstition. The pattern of the governess's narrative—whereby her unacknowledged personal rivalry takes the form of a public accusation—is, of course, precisely the pattern that was reenacted countless times in the Salem witch trials to which James makes reference. Victims of such accusations in colonial Salem were invariably marginal members of the community who had aroused the ire of their neighbors. Mere disagreeableness or personal eccentricity not being a capital offense even in colonial Salem, the offenders were typically accused of consorting with the devil.

James's recreation of this pattern in *The Turn of the Screw* contains two ironic "turns" of its own. First, although the governess brings her accusation against the ghosts of Peter Quint and Miss Jessel—both of whom are already dead—it is Miles, whose fundamental innocence she vehemently proclaims, who must die in their place. Second, she confides her accusation against the ghosts—not, as in a witch trial, to a public tribunal—but to her manuscript. The community of listeners, absent from the main story, is to be found, rather, in the frame tale, where it takes the form of Douglas's listeners, who anticipate the pleasure of imagining the sufferings of innocent children. The ostensibly private nature of the governess's experiences at Bly tends to distract attention from its ultimately public dimension. She does, however, leave behind a manuscript containing a version of events that effectively indicts Peter Quint and Miss Jessel in the eyes of her readers. The several theatrical metaphors that appear in her narrative, which I mentioned earlier in connection with *Guy Domville*, con-

vey the idea of her performing for an imaginary audience, as does
her vision of herself as a solitary ship's captain who must perform
heroically in the eyes of a handful of passengers.

Douglas's listeners will, in their turn, replicate the behavior of the
community itself in the sense that they willingly participate in a public ceremony involving the suffering of designated victims among
whom they will not themselves be numbered. Douglas assures his audience that the "dreadful" experience that he is about to recount
was not—"Oh thank God, no!" (146)—his own. The audience is likewise guaranteed that such suffering as they are likely to experience
will be purely vicarious—the suffering of one child in the first story,
then of two children in Douglas's, but never, "thank God," their own.
Thus, the governess's seemingly solitary act of bringing an accusation against figures whom she designates as moral reprobates is
shadowed in the frame tale by an audience that is ready to respond
appreciatively to the suffering of someone other than its members.
The pattern of collective persecution, which the psychological focus
of her narrative serves both to repress and to embody in a disguised
form, appears directly and explicitly when the governess asks herself
"who would ever absolve me, who would consent that *I should go un-
hung*" (204; my italics) if she violated the terms of her relationship
with Miles.

So also the circumstances of Miles's death seem to preclude our
attributing to it a public significance: he dies from heart failure
rather than a lynching. In this respect, he may remind us of Jay
Gatsby, the circumstances of whose death likewise point to a purely
private event. As we shall see in the chapter on Fitzgerald's novel,
however, Nick Carraway does allude to an implicit ritualistic pattern
when he describes Gatsby's death as a "holocaust." Similarly, the
death of Miles—which occurs in the privacy of a room at Bly, and
with the governess as sole witness—inevitably recalls the public ostracism that occurred when he was expelled from his boarding
school. Not surprisingly perhaps, the governess, who "knows" beyond any doubt that the headmaster of the school is "unspeakably
vile," does not see in her own effect on Miles consequences that
replicate, though in a genuinely tragic way, those that followed the
decision of her despised yet emulated predecessor.

It is interesting, when reflecting on the incident of Miles's expulsion, to notice that the question that it raises—both for the gov-

erness and for her readers, who dutifully mimic her behavior—
concerns only the behavior of Miles himself. What could he possibly
have done to merit such drastic punishment, we all ask. When the
governess does finally interrogate him on this point, she succeeds
only in drawing from him the enigmatic admission: "Well—I said
things" (259). Subsequent questioning elicits only the further detail
that Miles said these "things" only to a few schoolmates—"Those I
liked" (259). Most readers of *The Turn of the Screw*, following this
lead, assume predictably, and not unreasonably, that Miles was expelled for some unspecified sexual misdemeanor.

   This assumption, however, completely overlooks the question of
*communal* motivation that James implicitly raises from the opening
line of the frame tale, which gives us information relating to the behavior, not of an individual, but of a group of listeners whom he portrays as enjoying a morally equivocal form of entertainment. It also
ignores the fact that, whatever the details of Miles's behavior, his expulsion from his boarding school creates an uncanny mirroring relationship between himself and the governess, who was "expelled"
from her home as a result of her having been the youngest of her father's daughters. This rarely discussed detail implies that, even in
the complete absence of a legitimating accusation, human communities find it convenient to ostracize certain of their members.

   In the case of the governess, we may reasonably assume that her
family's motive was the time-honored one of diminishing the competition for limited resources within a family by reducing the number of its members. With respect to Miles, what he said (and what his
enigmatic words might be interpreted as telling us about his moral
character) may, ultimately, be less important than the reaction of the
boarding school itself, which has used his actions as a pretext for the
staging of a purificatory ritual. In this respect, the really crucial detail may not be Miles's moral failing but the implied vulnerability
that makes his expulsion an uproblematic event, perhaps even the
occasion of renewed solidarity, in the life of his school. Miles has behind him—not an influential and concerned guardian whose reaction the school must take into account—but only a feckless uncle.

   Finally, any effort to bring to light, or to imagine, the actual details of Miles's dereliction will necessarily overlook what we might
call the "constructive" effect that James achieves by excluding these
details from his novella. As the unnamed narrator's comment about

the greater compactness and selectness brought to the group of listeners by the "departing ladies" reminds us, excluded terms are not
necessarily to be thought of as missing pieces that need to be re-
stored in order that a puzzle can be completed or resolved. Rather,
they are elements whose absence produces an effect that requires,
not their eventual retrieval, but their continued exclusion. James
himself referred to this aspect of his tale when he said: So long as the
events are veiled, the imagination will run riot and depict all sorts of
horrors, but as soon as the veil is lifted, all mystery disappears"
(quoted by Edel in Esch and Warren, *Turn of the Screw,* 192). We may
remember in this regard that James had originally planned to tell his
story in a "tolerably obvious" way (in Esch and Warren, *Turn of the
Screw,* 112). His subsequent "expulsion" of the obvious thus produced the tale as we actually have it.

The characters, events, and explanations that James has expelled
from his tale must remain beyond the pale of the narrative itself.
Does any reader of *The Turn of the Screw,* for example, seriously wish
that the children's absentee uncle had suddenly appeared at Bly? Or
would any reader contend that James made a serious aesthetic mistake in staging the ghostly return of Miss Jessel and Peter Quint
rather than of Miles and Flora's parents? In a deeper way, does anyone wish that the governess possessed that sensitivity to ambiguities
and openness to diverse possible interpretations that she tendentiously excludes from her narrative? As James himself suggests in his
preface, the aura of mystery and pervasive evil with which he wanted
to imbue his/her narrative would have been entirely lost if he had
endowed her with this faculty. The formal features of the novella depend upon a type of narrative ostracism that, unlike the governess's
prosecutorial stance, does not imply any moral censure. James's
strategy in devising these exclusions is to stage the return of "the old
trials for witchcraft" in such a way as to demystify them by making exclusion an *aesthetic requirement* of the work itself rather than the sign
of a *moral defect.*

# 2

## *Heart of Darkness:*
## The Outsider Demystified

Lᴉᴋᴇ *Tʜᴇ Tᴜʀɴ ᴏꜰ ᴛʜᴇ Sᴄʀᴇᴡ,* Jᴏꜱᴇᴘʜ Cᴏɴʀᴀᴅ'ꜱ *Hᴇᴀʀᴛ ᴏꜰ Dᴀʀᴋɴᴇꜱꜱ* presents a fictional world in which foundational distinctions are no longer respected. The transgression of the boundary between the living and of the dead, which is the originary event of *The Turn of the Screw,* is recreated, in *Heart of Darkness,* by the dissolution of the boundary between "civilized" and "savage" peoples. Something of the ancient terror provoked by twins—whose likeness to each other deprives identity of its grounding in reciprocal differences—lurks behind each novel.[1] The ghosts, as we saw in the preceding chapter, prove to be, disquietingly, mirror images of the governess herself; likewise, Marlow will, in the course of his journey up the Congo River, encounter "savages" who bear an uncanny resemblance to himself as well as to his fellow Europeans.

Marlow and the governess are also alike in that they belong and, at the same time, do not belong to the communities in which we find them; both of them will, in consequence, attempt to strengthen their claim to communal membership by resorting to scapegoating. Since the governess does not belong unproblematically to the world of Bly, she attempts to assert her right to be there by insisting upon her superiority to the morally odious ghosts. Likewise, Marlow is at a disadvantage in his relation to the listeners gathered aboard the *Nellie;* as the unnamed narrator pointedly tells us, Marlow "did not represent his class" (18). Along with his failure to adopt the normally sedentary life of the seaman, Marlow does not tell his yarns in the approved manner. Like the governess, he will seek to bond with a community to which he does not naturally belong by appealing to their shared fear, or disdain, of certain outsiders who belong to this community even less than he does. Conrad, however, complicates the strategy that we saw at work in *The Turn of the Screw* by making Marlow ostensibly the friend and admirer of the figures that he otherwise tends to scapegoat.

The frame tales of both novels will, in their turn, point toward nonsacrificial resolutions of the central conflict presented in the main story. In *The Turn of the Screw*, the unacknowledged rivalry that leads the governess to transform the ghosts into the privileged victims of her persecution narrative is resolved by Douglas's performative and creative use of the ghost that the governess has become for him. In a similar way, the idolatry that distorts both Marlow's and the natives' relationships with Kurtz will be resolved in the frame tale, where the unnamed narrator's assertion that Marlow "resembled an idol" (16) stages the return of a Kurtz-like figure but in a way that arouses skepticism rather than producing a worshipful attitude.

Analysis of the relationship between the frame tale and the main story will help us to appreciate the degree to which Conrad demystifies the mythic belief in the distinguishing traits that Marlow tendentiously attributes to his designated outsiders. It will also prepare us to see that he projects, in the frame tale, an alternative response to anxieties about a "remote kinship" that does not rely upon the now-discredited procedure through which the "other"—whether deified or disdained—is constructed. Instead of relying upon recourse to the ideology of racial (or gender) superiority, Conrad locates a real and sustaining difference in the distance between the mythologized figures that Marlow constructs throughout his narrative and the demystified figure of Marlow himself, who creates bonds among the members of his community without becoming its scapegoat.

This substitutive role of the storyteller is in accord with Conrad's own comments on the purposes of art, which repeatedly affirm the prophetic nature of the artist's relation to his community. For Conrad, the artist is above all someone who "speaks to our capacity for delight and wonder, to the sense of mystery surrounding our lives . . . to the latent feeling of fellowship with all creation—and to the subtle but invincible, conviction of solidarity that knits together the loneliness of innumerable hearts" (*Criticism*, 145–46). In *Heart of Darkness* he presents the activity of the storyteller as a sublimated alternative to the violent, atavistic methods for achieving solidarity to which human communities are otherwise likely to resort. He further associates storytelling with the gradual unfolding of truth by subjecting the story of Kurtz to three consecutive retellings: first, Marlow's account to the Intended, in which he consciously suppresses Kurtz's final words; second, the account that he gives to his listeners aboard the *Nellie*, in which he only partially glimpses the true meaning of his stories; third, the virtual reading, not as yet achieved by any of the novel's subsequent readers, in which its true meaning is fully revealed.[2]

A decisive step toward this final revelation was achieved by the Nigerian novelist Chinua Achebe, who, in "An Image of Africa: Racism in Conrad's *Heart of Darkness*," made two related assertions about the novel that significantly advance its interpretation.[3] Achebe argued, in the first place, that Conrad's image of Africa is not merely an expression of personal prejudice; rather, it serves the rhetorical purpose of establishing a bond between the author and his readers: "But Conrad chose his subject well—one which was guaranteed not to put him in conflict with the psychological pre-disposition of his readers" (in Kimbrough, *Heart of Darkness*, 253). There can be little doubt that throughout his narrative Marlow does count on the readiness of his all-white audience aboard the *Nellie* to think of black Africans as different from themselves. When he refers to a character as a "Buck Nigger" or, in another example cited by Achebe, calls redundant attention to the blackness of a particular African, we may assume that none of his listeners is an African, or, for that matter, a member of any other minority. Throughout his narrative, the African continent itself is portrayed as a feminine "other," a metaphoric comparison from which we may deduce that Marlow's listeners are not only all white, but also all male.[4]

Achebe also points to the fact that the anxieties that shape Marlow's narrative are of a collective, rather than a merely individual, nature. Africa, as portrayed by Conrad through Marlow, plays, for the community of his Western readers, the perennial role of the scapegoat:

> As I said earlier, Conrad did not originate the image of Africa which we find in his book. It was and is the dominant image of Africa in the Western imagination and Conrad merely brought the peculiar gifts of his own mind to bear on it.

> For reasons which can certainly use close psychological in-
> quiry, the West seems to suffer deep anxieties about the pre-
> cariousness of its civilization and to have a need for constant
> reassurance by comparing it with Africa. If Europe, advancing
> in civilization, could cast a backward glance periodically at
> Africa trapped in primordial barbarity, it could say with faith
> and feeling: There go I but for the grace of God. Africa is to
> Europe as the picture is to Dorian Gray—a carrier onto whom
> the master unloads his physical and moral deformities so that
> he may go forward erect and immaculate. Consequently,
> Africa is something to be avoided just as the picture has to be
> hidden away to safeguard the man's jeopardous integrity. (in
> Kimbrough, *Heart of Darkness*, 261)

Achebe's analysis of the transformation of Africa into a scapegoat
(what he himself calls a "carrier") needs, however, to be significantly
qualified before its value can be fully appreciated. Achebe is surely
right in pointing to the scapegoating mechanism as the underlying
pattern of *Heart of Darkness*. His own personal, and entirely reasonable, concern for the portrayal of Africa in the novel leads him, however, to ignore other groups or individuals toward whom this
mechanism is directed. Achebe assumes, in particular, that this "carrier" must necessarily be an object of contempt, which explains why
he overlooks Marlow's equally characteristic resort to *admiration* as
he constructs his outsiders, of which the most dubious example appears in his glowing portrayal of British imperialism.

The role of the scapegoat in Conrad's novel can be played, not
only by black Africans who perform "unspeakable rites," but also
women, because they are "out of touch with reality," and by Kurtz
himself, both because he is a "prodigy" and because he "lacked restraint" to an exemplary degree. The crucial feature in the choice of
an object of scapegoating is not, as Achebe maintains, race, but
rather Marlow's capacity to believe in the real, essential distinctive-
ness of these designated others. Shadowing Marlow's repeated constructions and reconstructions of others throughout his narrative is,
however, the lurking fear that they may not, after all, be as different
as he would like to imagine them.

Marlow's premonition of a "remote kinship" (63) between the
starkly differentiated elements of his narrative itself points to his fear

of a world that, lacking credible others (because the presumptive candidates all look unsettlingly like oneself) would succumb to a chaotic loss of differentiation. Because Marlow is specifically talking about Africans when he raises this possibility of this disquieting kinship, Achebe narrowly interprets his remark as an expression of racist superiority. However, we need only remember Marlow's suspicion that women must remain in their "beautiful world" lest our own become worse to realize, first, that race is not the crucial element of his mythology and, second, that he fears not merely the humiliating discovery of his similarity to a presumably inferior being, but, rather, some not clearly specified catastrophe that would follow upon the loss of distinction between their "beautiful world" and the world of "facts" that he attributes to himself and his listeners. The distinctions to which Marlow has recourse are surely factitious; the traumatic encounter with a world from which all distinctions have vanished—which Marlow describes at one point as an "impalpable greyness" (113)—is, however, entirely real. His recounting of this experience requires a skeptical, but also a respectful, hearing.

Regardless of the specific identity of either the designated individual or of the group that designates him, the nature of the relationship and its outcome is entirely predictable: the group will be shown repeatedly as using its outsider to create a sense of solidarity. Its members will either worship this figure as unutterably superior to themselves or subject him to some "unspeakable rite" whereby he becomes the object of their aggressive instincts. Kurtz, of course, provokes both responses in *Heart of Darkness*: worshiped by the natives who try to retain him in their midst, he at the same time provokes the disdain of the company, which wants to remove him from his prominent position within its hierarchy. Both of these communal responses to Kurtz are then replicated by Marlow, who finds him to be both "the most "exalted and the most contemptible" of men (79). In the climactic scene with the Intended, Marlow will both exalt Kurtz—"He was a remarkable man" (120)—and expel him by suppressing his final words.

Marlow's parallel exaltation of women begins with his allusion to the "Parcae" whom he meets at the company's office in the form of "[t]wo women, one fat and the other slim [who] sat on straw-bottomed chairs, knitting black wool" (24). The "great man" that Marlow meets here in the person of the company director—"He was five feet six, I should judge" (25)—does not possess physical stature equal to the epithet that Marlow bestows upon him with obvious irony. In contrast, the women become—through a somewhat heavy-handed process of archetypal inflation that prefigures Marlow's later characterization of Kurtz—uncannily supernatural beings:

> Two youths with foolish and cheery countenances were being piloted over, and she threw at them the same quick glance of unconcerned wisdom. She seemed to know all about them and about me too. An eerie feeling came over me. She seemed uncanny and fateful. Often far away there I thought of these two, guarding the door of Darkness, knitting wool as for a warm pall, one introducing continuously to the unknown, the other scrutinising the cheery and foolish faces with uncon-cerned eyes. *Ave!* Old knitter of black wool. *Morituri te saluant.* Not many of those she looked at ever saw her again—not half, by a long way. (26)

When he visits his aunt, Marlow will adopt the opposed (yet funda-mentally equivalent) strategy of inviting his listeners to condescend to her in a way that affirms their own male superiority: "It's queer how out of touch with truth women are. They live in a world of their own, and there had never been anything like it, and never can be. It is too beautiful altogether, and if they were to set it up it would go to pieces before the first sunset. Some confounded fact we men have been living contentedly with ever since the day of creation would start up and knock the whole thing over" (28).

Whether exalted or derided, women *must*, for Marlow, inhabit "a world of their own" if his own masculine world is to maintain a sem-blance of stability and coherence. They are like the blank spaces on the maps of his childhood memories, which must remain "other" in order that men—whether "foolish and cheery" or "living content-edly" with their facts—can be defined in contrast to them. Kurtz's mistress will be assigned to these blank spaces, thanks, not to any in-herent qualities that she might possess but, rather, to Marlow's mythologizing characterization of her as "a wild and gorgeous ap-parition of a woman" (99). Every detail of his description of her is, as Achebe has rightly observed, patently intended to portray her as ab-solutely unlike any of Marlow's listeners:

She walked with measured steps, draped in striped and fringed cloths, treading the earth proudly, with a slight jingle and flash of barbarous ornaments. She carried her head high; her hair was done in the shape of a helmet; she had brass leggings to the knee, brass wire gauntlets to the elbow, a crimson spot on her tawny cheek, innumerable necklaces of glass beads on her neck; bizarre things, charms, gifts of witch-men, that hung about her, glittered and trembled at every step. She must have had the value of several elephant tusks upon her. She was savage and superb, wild-eyed and magnificent; there was something ominous and stately in her deliberate progress. And in the hush that had fallen suddenly upon the whole sorrowful land, the immense wilderness, the colossal body of the fecund and mysterious life seemed to look at her, pensive, as though it had been looking at the image of its own tenebrous and passionate soul. (99)

At the end of his narrative, Marlow's description of Kurtz's Intended—"This fair hair, this pale visage, this pure brow, seemed surrounded by an ashy halo from which the dark eyes looked out at me" (119)—betrays a mythologizing impulse to maintain the belief in the real existence of mysterious places or beings that was first awakened in him by the blank spaces of the cartographers. Like these heretofore unmapped regions, women, Kurtz and cannibals serve as equivalents of "a white patch for a boy to dream gloriously over" (22).

Readers of *Heart of Darkness* have always noticed that Marlow's journey to his meeting with Kurtz and cannibalism has symbolic implications that far exceed the practical purposes that it serves. Psychological readings, which interpret his trip up the river as a journey into the darker regions of Marlow's psyche, have been particularly numerous. Albert Guerard offered the classic statement of this approach in *Conrad the Novelist,* where he argues that the trip up the river amounts to "a spiritual voyage of self-discovery" (244). More recently, Peter Firchow has noted that the historical quest for the sources of the Nile, in which we may see an avatar of Marlow's own journey, already possessed this spiritual dimension in that sense that it "represented more powerfully than anything else . . . the quest for a 'final' symbolic answer to the question of who we are." As he also reminds us, "not only for Conrad but also for contemporaneous Eu-

ropean writers as different as Gustave Flaubert and H. Rider Hag-
gard, envisioning Africa in fiction became an analogue for the ex-
ploration of the hidden, dark regions of their inner selves" (20). In
an interpretation of the significance of Marlow's journey to the Central Station that is closer to my own approach, Peter Brooks sees it
more as a structural requirement of the novel than as an expression
of Marlow's personal psychology. The purpose of Marlow's journey,
according to Brooks, is "to detect the meaning and the consequences of Kurtz's return upriver" (*Reading for the Plot*, 244). He sees
this journey as a "belated" repetition of Kurtz's, one whose activity of
"uncovering and constructing the meaning and the authority of the
narrative represents the very process of narrative representation"
(245).

Brooks's analysis of the repetitions that underlie both Marlow's
journey and his subsequent narrative (as well as the potentially infi-
nite series of repeated acts of reading and interpretation that the
novel itself invites) marks a decisive stage in interpretation of *Heart
of Darkness*. Brooks does not, however, relate the repetitive structure
of the novel to its underlying scapegoating pattern. In order to make
this connection, we must notice that Marlow's journey repeats, not
only Kurtz's earlier journey, but his own preliminary journey to the
company's station, which had led him to the "grove of death" and,
thus, to the discovery of European depravity. Brooks emphasizes the
belatedness of Marlow's journey with respect to Kurtz's and the resulting "perpetual slippage of meaning" (259) that will continually
defeat any attempt to impose closure on his narrative or on its interpretation by successive readers. We may, however, argue that Conrad
sends Marlow up the river, not so much in order that he discover the
elusive meaning of his predecessor's own journey, but so that he can
find a "carrier"—an equivalent of the picture of Dorian Gray that
Achebe had evoked—upon whom to disburden the depravity that
he had discovered in the "grove of death." Marlow's journey leads
him not only to Kurtz but to his encounter with cannibalistic practices. These rituals, and Kurtz's participation in them, provide Marlow with the reassuring conviction (however delusive we may judge
this, finally, to be) that the horrendous cruelty of the Europeans
does not represent evil in its purest and most appalling form. The
final stage in his journey into that particular heart of darkness does
not occur until he witnesses the "unspeakable rites" practiced jointly

by a community of black Africans and a solitary white European.

Tony C. Brown has pertinently observed that *Heart of Darkness* contains a fundamental ambiguity in its portrayal of evil, what he describes as "an obscure vacillation between the horror as an effect of colonial intervention and the location of the horror's cause in the environment itself" ("Cultural Psychosis," 17). This hesitation between ascribing the horror to African primitivism or to European colonialism creates an ambiguity whereby the *setting* in which evil manifests itself is discovered to be its *cause*. Brown's analysis of the "unspeakable rites" as a repetition—albeit one that is not consciously acknowledged by Marlow—of his encounter with evil in the "grove of death" clearly points to the presence of an underlying scapegoating mechanism. The relationship between the two scenes involves, not simply a repetition, but a *displacement* whereby the barbarous behavior of the Europeans becomes a merely preparatory stage to Marlow's encounter with the ultimate savagery represented by cannibalistic rituals themselves as well as by Kurtz's own moral collapse.

It is symptomatic of the fundamentally mythic nature of this process of displacement that Marlow must resort to an exceptionally strenuous display of rhetorical overkill in order to render it:

> The monotonous beating of a big drum filled the air with muffled shocks and a lingering vibration. A steady droning sound of many men chanting each to himself some weird incantation came out from the black, flat wall of the woods as the humming of bees comes out of a hive, and had a strange narcotic effect upon my half-awake senses. I believe I dozed off leaning over the rail, till an abrupt burst of yells, an overwhelming outbreak of a pent-up and mysterious frenzy, woke me up in a bewildered wonder" (104).

His subsequent report on the ceremony likewise involves a choice of words whose purpose is to stress its utter unlikeness to anything for which his European experience has prepared him: "A black figure stood up, strode on long black legs, waving long black arms, across the glow. It had horns—antelope horns, I think—on its head. Some sorcerer, some witch-man, no doubt: it looked fiend-like enough" (106). Marlow's warning to Kurtz—"You will be lost . . . utterly lost" (106)—appropriately intimates that the depths of evil represented by this ceremony have no common measure with the iniquities of the colonizing mission that first brought Kurtz to Africa.

At some point in our reflection of Marlow's strategy, however, we must recognize that he is not simply *describing* a primitive ritual; he is, rather, *enacting* a ritual that constructs Africans as a reassuring scapegoat for both himself and the community formed by his European listeners. Achebe rightly points to the fact that, at such moments as these, Conrad is "engaged in inducing hypnotic stupor in his readers through a bombardment of emotive words and other forms of trickery" (in Kimbrough, *Heart of Darkness,* 253). His comment also applies to Marlow's description of Kurtz's own moral corruption. Unlike Dante who, in the original *Inferno* of which *Heart of Darkness* is a conscious rewriting, subjected the moral failings of its inhabitants to a rigorously objective analysis, Marlow constantly employs vague generalities that point, not so much to the precise nature of Kurtz's moral failings, as to his own need to construct them, whatever they are, as fundamentally incommensurate with the atrocities committed by the other Europeans. Thus, although Marlow appears to have deprived us of the eyewitness account of the "unspeakable rites" to which we may have felt entitled, he does create, before our very eyes as it were, an analogous ritual to which we have become unwitting yet complicitous observers.

The problem with Marlow's account of the cannibalistic rituals is that the skeptical reader (in the absence of a proper epilogue, we do not know if there were any skeptical *listeners*) is likely to feel that nothing—not even cannibalism or human sacrifice—could possibly be significantly more horrifying than the spectacle of the dying African laborers that Marlow had already described with great objectivity in the "grove of death":

> They were dying slowly—it was very clear. They were not enemies, they were not criminals, they were nothing earthly now,—nothing but black shadows of disease and starvation, lying confusedly in the greenish gloom. Brought from all the recesses of the coast in all the legality of time contracts, lost in uncongenial surroundings, fed on unfamiliar food, they sickened, became inefficient, and were then allowed to crawl away and rest. These moribund shapes were free as air—and nearly as thin. I began to distinguish the gleam of eyes under the trees. Then glancing down, I saw a face near my hand. The

black bones reclined at full length with one shoulder against the tree, and slowly the eyelids rose and the sunken eyes looked up at me, enormous and vacant, a kind of blind, white flicker in the depths of the orbs, which died out slowly. (35)

Significantly, Marlow does not need to resort to the obfuscating language that he used in his portrayal of the "unspeakable rites" in order to convey the moral significance of this scene. The details alone provide the appropriate commentary.

Frances B. Singh, who perceptively analyzes the scapegoating process that is ironically at work in Marlow's presentation of cannibalism as the ultimate horror, has argued that Marlow "refuses to become enlightened about the significance of these customs, remaining transfixed by the surface horror they generate for the European. He calls them 'unspeakable,' says on one occasion, 'I don't want to know anything of the ceremonies used when approaching Mr. Kurtz,' and believes as an article of faith that Kurtz will be 'utterly lost' if he participates in a certain ceremony" (in Kimbrough, *Heart of Darkness,* 272). Singh further points out that "Marlow's ignorance here with respect to the habits of cannibals is noteworthy . . . what he should have realized, if he had really kept his eyes and mind open, was that cannibals do not eat human flesh out of greed or lust or even as a dietary staple, but to commemorate an important occasion connected with the well-being of their society" (274–75). She concludes that Marlow makes cannibalism a convenient "carrier" of his own unavowable impulses:

But there is no indication that apart from what Marlow says these rites are being performed so as to invoke the dark powers. Therefore if Marlow is feeling the call of the wild in these ceremonies it is because he has invested them with it in the first place. It is as if Marlow, not able to cope with his guilt feelings about possessing unsocial drives and urges, transfers them to a perfectly innocent, though apparently fearsome, group of people, and labels them as devotees of the powers of darkness because (1) that way he can get out of thinking that they and he are both human, (2) that way he can blame somebody else for his own problems, and (3) the connection between physical blackness and psychical darkness is only too easy to make and believe in. (275)

Singh limits her analysis of scapegoating to examples involving spurious European stereotypes about "primitive peoples" that are conveyed by *Heart of Darkness*. She could, however, have extended her analysis to include discussion of the ways in which Marlow equally constructs Kurtz as a scapegoat (a fact to which she implicitly alludes in her remark about Marlow's "unsocial drives").

As Ian Glenn has shown, Marlow's portrayal of Kurtz incorporates certain Victorian prejudices with regard to the figure of the "bohemian artist." In stressing the artistic and intellectual side of Kurtz, Glenn argues, "Conrad was dramatizing a fairly typical conservative fear of deracinated intellectuals" ("Conrad's *Heart of Darkness*,"239). In the process of substantiating his argument, Glenn calls attention to the fact that, as Marlow learns more about him, "Kurtz, no longer the efficient agent, member of the 'gang of virtue,' has become more specifically an intellectual or artist than a moral figure, but inextricably connected with this is the discovery that he is also someone who has murdered and lost all restraint, someone who threatens the safety of those on board the steamer" (243). Kurtz's moral dissolution in the African wilderness thus represents, according to Glenn, the symbolic means whereby Conrad dramatizes "the consequences of a liberated intellectual and artistic practice that in his view threatens the existing social order" (245).

Glenn's subsequent observation that Marlow represents a positive image of the artist/intellectual who had been negatively portrayed by Kurtz points, in a way that is consonant with Singh's discussion of the scapegoating of cannibals, to the process of displacement whereby Marlow projects upon Kurtz disquieting aspects of himself. In order to appreciate the significance of Glenn's analysis, we need to remember that traditional interpretations of Marlow's encounter with Kurtz tended to treat it narrowly in individual and psychological terms. Guerard, for example, described *Heart of Darkness* as recounting "the night journey into the unconscious, and confrontation of an entity within the self" (*Conrad the Novelist*, 245). As Glenn makes clear, however, this neutrally described "entity" is actually a stereotyped figure (the artist/intellectual as threat to the social order) whom Marlow could count upon to arouse the antipathy of his listeners. In retrospect, his analysis points to the ethically troubling undertones of Guerard's assertion that Kurtz was, for Marlow, "a potential and fallen self" (244), a characterization whose sacrificial implications Guerard himself would surely not have intended.

Marlow is not, however, only repelled by the spectacle of Kurtz's moral degradation; he also regards him as an exceptionally exalted figure in whom he may contemplate certain positive qualities that he himself lacks. In the absence of compelling empirical evidence in support of his psychologically necessary claim that Kurtz was a "remarkable" man, Marlow attempts to base this assertion on the moral triumph that he attributes to Kurtz's final words. Kurtz himself provides no gloss on this cry—"The horror! The horror!" (112) —nor do we have an omniscient narrator ready to interpret this enigmatic phrase in a convincingly unequivocal way. The ambiguity of the phrase allows Marlow to find in it not so much what is actually there as what he needs to believe.

As Vincent Pecora has observed, Marlow's predilection for investing Kurtz's words with special significance is given strong encouragement by the societal elevation of the words of a dying man: "For the dying man's last words, if time has permitted them, will come after his life has passed before him, after he has had the opportunity to review and pass judgement; in their autonomous moral elevation, they represent a final kind of self-knowledge that allows the individual to recognize the truth of his existence, and that provides a means of moral rectification for his society. This is indeed a process that earlier criticism readily described as central in countless nineteenth-century novels" ("Phenomenology of Voice," 1001). While the meaning of Kurtz's words cannot be ascertained with any degree of certainty, Marlow's commentary, once stripped of its claims to authority, offers us a quite revealing insight into the psychological need that generates the interpretation as well as of the societal impulse that condones it. Having ambiguously denigrated and elevated the Intended, as well as his aunt, for reasons that are easily decipherable, he then responds to Kurtz in obedience to a similarly self-protective reflex that mimics the behavior of the natives.

Marlow admires Kurtz because his own near-death experience robbed him of the power of speech. Kurtz, on the contrary, spoke words that amounted to a moral triumph: "I was within a hair's breadth of the last opportunity for pronouncement, and found with humiliation that probably I would have nothing to say. This is the

reason why I affirm that Kurtz was a remarkable man. He had something to say" (113). Like Dante lost in the dark wood, Marlow recognizes his own inability to defend himself against the darkness. Thus,
Kurtz magically appears as a rescuing figure who assures the lost one
that while he is also there in the dark wood he knows his way back to
the light. Kurtz's final words, their ambiguity notwithstanding, have
for Marlow the mark of invulnerability; they prove that language,
when spoken with sufficiently imputed authority, can withstand the
darkness. In this episode, however, Marlow is constructing Kurtz just
as he will later construct the Intended. Needing a life ring as he sinks
into the darkness, he decides that Kurtz has thrown one to him. Essentially, the role of the rescuer is to assure the one that he rescues
that the darkness that engulfs him is not the sole reality. He—and
perhaps even more pertinently the words that he speaks—bears witness to the existence of an alternative realm that is every bit as real
as, and even more powerful than, the encompassing darkness. This
aspect of Marlow's response to Kurtz mimics the attitude of the
African natives who, as Kurtz himself explains in his report, have invested in him "the might as of a deity" (83).

As Peter Brooks has remarked, Marlow seems to envision Kurtz as
a commanding paternal figure "whose final articulation transmits
wisdom" (*Reading for the Plot*, 248). His putative status as a symbolic
father, one who has been blessed with the gift of language, serves to
assure Marlow that the return of infantile dependency upon a dominant maternal figure is not the only option. Many details of *Heart of
Darkness*—such as his abashed admission that he owed his position
with the company to his aunt's influence—support the idea that
Marlow fears precisely the contrary proof of his inescapable dependency. An equally telling revelation of his fear of feminine power occurs during his interview at the company office, where he notices the
two women who are knitting. As Peter Hyland has observed: "[Mar-
low] is disturbed by them because they seem to know all about him;
he feels himself to be in their hands without knowing how" ("Little
Woman," 10).

Numerous images in *Heart of Darkness* portray the jungle, in turn,
as an enticing, yet perhaps also menacing, maternal figure. At one
point, Marlow compares it to a nurturing breast: "afterwards he [a
"nigger" who had been beaten] arose and went out—and the wilderness without a sound took him into its bosom again" (45). Later, the

ambivalent connotations of the jungle will be suggested by a metaphor that links it to the sea when Marlow describes the Eldorado Expedition as going "into the patient wilderness, that closed upon it as
the sea closes over a diver" (59). The menacing aspect of the jungle—its capacity for provoking a frightening return of infantile pow-
erlessness—is foregrounded by Marlow's description of the effect
produced by the night: "it seemed unnatural, like a state of trance.
Not the faintest sound of any kind could be heard . . . then the night
came suddenly, and struck you blind as well" (67). In a related way,
Marlow resorts to a maternal metaphor when he says of Kurtz that
"[t]he wilderness had patted him on the head . . . caressed him . . .
taken him, loved him, embraced him" (81) and, even more clearly,
when he describes him as "opening his mouth voraciously, as if to devour all the earth with all its mankind" (117). According to Marlow,
however, Kurtz is not reduced to utter infantilism; rather, he becomes magically transformed into the idealized paternal figure that
Marlow needs to protect him from the darkness. His mouth, which
would devour everything, also speaks words that identify him with a
linguistic realm that possesses an independent reality.

Conrad implicitly demystifies Marlow's construction of Kurtz as a
"remarkable" figure, however, by placing in *Heart of Darkness* at least
one scene that, while not appreciably forwarding the plot, does reveal a blatant act of misinterpretation that reflects prospectively on
Marlow's own. This occurs when Marlow talks with the brick maker,
who has apparently convinced himself that Marlow is a person of influence. Despite his disdain for lies, Marlow allows the brick maker
"to believe anything he liked to imagine as to my influence in Europe" (50). Marlow recognizes in this episode that he has become
the target of wishful projections from which he has no difficulty in
detaching himself: "I became in an instant as much of a pretence as
the rest of the bewitched pilgrims" (50). His detachment permits
Marlow to condescend to the brick maker, who fails to recognize
that the "prominent" Marlow with whom he believes himself to be
speaking is, in fact, merely a projection of his own needs. The brick
maker is deluded because he imagines that Marlow has influence
with powerful people; Marlow, however, recognizes that there is
nothing substantial behind the imaginary construction that he has
become: "And there was nothing behind me! There was nothing but
that wretched, old, mangled steamboat I was leaning against" (51).

The irony is that, having demystified idolatry during an episode in which he was made its object, Marlow is decidedly less alert when, in his encounter with Kurtz, it is he who falls victim to illusions.

Conrad makes Marlow a victim of the novel's irony once again when he sets his narrator's confident interpretation of Kurtz's final words against the background of his pervasively uncertain responses to nearly every other episode of his journey.[5] He is, for example, unsure as to what significance he should attach to his sunken steamship: "I fancy I see it now, but I am not sure—not at all" (41). Likewise, he finds statements made by the company manager obscure, particularly because of the latter's habit of concluding his speeches with an enigmatic smile: "It came at the end of his speeches like a seal applied on the words to make the meaning of the commonest phrase appear absolutely inscrutable" (41). Later, when he discovers that Kurtz, after coming partway down the river, has suddenly decided to return to the Inner Station, he is left clueless as to the significance of this decision. The most revelatory of these episodes occurs when he observes the piece of "white worsted" material worn by the young black man who is dying in the "grove of death." Marlow wonders "[w]as it a badge—an ornament—a charm —a propitiatory act? Was there any idea at all connected with it?" (35). Like the conversation with the brick maker, this episode provides a parallel to Marlow's listening to Kurtz's last words. In both cases a signifying sign—a repeated phrase in one case, a piece of cloth in the other—seems to Marlow to have something behind it. The meaning of both signs is equally obscure; Kurtz's words are at least as subject to interpretation as the white worsted material, yet Marlow is confident in his interpretation of the one but left perplexed by the other.

The difference between the two episodes lies not in the objectively observable features of each sign, but in Marlow's greater need to attach a reassuring interpretation to Kurtz's words. The cloth tied around the black man's neck presents Marlow with a merely momentary and peripheral challenge. He must interpret Kurtz's words, however, in such a way as to sustain his belief in the latter's uniqueness. Kurtz's words thus bear the burden of affirming the unquestionable existence of an alternative realm inhabited by someone who is, unquestionably, an outsider. Marlow's way of interpreting them is an entirely comprehensible psychological response to the threat of a defeat from which there would be no recourse. A similarly mythologizing process is at work when Marlow visits Kurtz's Intended. In that scene, his construction of the young woman as a superior being and his subsequent refusal to divulge Kurtz's actual last words are based on a belief that seems more the expression of some deeply felt need on his own part than on a legitimate inference from experience. In short, he claims that, as a woman, she must be protected from the truth about Kurtz's self-inflicted degradation. There is good reason, however, to believe that Marlow is the more likely candidate for such protection and that his perception of her is designed to provide him, albeit a bit late, with precisely the safeguard that failed to appear during his own encounter with the darkness. His casting her in the role of the outsider allows him to form a bond with his male listeners, much as he had done earlier in condescending to his aunt.

The characteristic obtuseness of Marlow's observations on women have been well documented and analyzed by several feminist scholars. Nina Pelikan Straus correctly notes that the exclusion of women contributes significantly to the bonding that occurs aboard the *Nellie:* "Marlow speaks in *Heart of Darkness* to other men, and although he speaks about women, there is no indication that women might be included among his hearers, nor that his existence depends upon his 'hanging together' with a 'humanity' that includes the second sex" ("Exclusion of the Intended," 124). She further speculates that "[t]he peculiar density and inaccessibility of *Heart of Darkness* may be the result of its extremely masculine historical referentiality, its insistence on a male circle of readers" (124). This leads her to conclude that the implied comparison between Prometheus and Marlow, who like his classical prototype brings the truth to humanity at great risk is ultimately unfounded because "[u]nlike Prometheus, . . . Marlow brings truth to men by virtue of his bringing falsehood to women. Heroic maleness is defined precisely in adverse relation to delusional femininity" (129-30).

Similarly, Johanna Smith, borrowing from Hélène Cixous, argues that Marlow's narrative, like Kurtz's report to the society, is "a mystification of power relations" that serve to consign women to the realm of mystery" (in Murfin, *Heart of Darkness,* 183). Smith applies this principle to analyses of the chief accountant's native laundress, Kurtz's mistress, the jungle itself, the women at the company's office,

Marlow's aunt (in whose rhetoric she rightly sees a parallel with Kurtz's) and, finally, the Intended. Her analysis of Marlow's lie to the Intended leads to the conclusion, congruent with my own, that it should be interpreted as a self-protective gesture through which he projects upon a woman an emotional need for belief that he finds unworthy in himself as a man.

In revealing the constructed quality of the "beautiful world" that Marlow reserves for women, however, Smith noticeably omits mention of Kurtz as the third term of the "too *different* altogether" realm upon which Marlow's ideological vision of reality rather shakily rests. Furthermore, although she notes the striking similarity between the aunt's rhetoric and Kurtz's, she does not consider the possibility that Conrad might deserve credit for having introduced this destabilizing element into his novel. More generally, she fails to see that Conrad has constructed his novel in such a way that the single alternative realm inhabited by Africans, women, and Kurtz is revealed, once the distorting lens of Marlow's "vision" is removed, as a mirror image of the "closed male circle" to which Marlow has been speaking. This circle is composed of men who perform "unspeakable rites," who justify their actions through recourse to vacuous rationalizations, and who, in this way, engage in behavior that Marlow wants uniquely to attribute to his outsiders.

Marlow's constant, mystifying resort to unfounded differences is also at work in the distinction that he maintains between forms of violence that are legitimated by an ennobling idea and those that are not. He first introduces this distinction when, in the course of reflecting on the unrestrained brutality of the Europeans, he is led to moderate his moral revulsion against their cruelty by the thought that "[w]hat redeems it is the idea only. An idea at the back of it; not a sentimental pretence but an idea" (20). Marlow does not, however, clarify the distinction between an "idea" and a "sentimental pretence," nor do the events of the novel support the conclusion that the distinction itself is ultimately tenable. Probably the most transparent of his failed attempts to maintain this dichotomy occurs when, in the midst of his critique of the Eldorado Exploring Expedition, he tells us that their manner of speaking was "reckless without hardihood, greedy without audacity, and cruel without courage" (54–55). The irony of this critique surely lies in its assumption that the vices attributed to the pilgrims could, theoretically, be redeemed by the virtues to which he alludes. The Marlow who could earlier contemplate "the redeeming facts of life" only by turning his back on the Company Station might have recognized the ideological nature of this view. Instead, he allows himself to become the spokesman for the belief that violence can be justified by the values that it presumably serves.

Perhaps the deepest irony of *Heart of Darkness* lies in Marlow's failure to recognize that there is, finally, no substantive distinction between the company's repudiation of Kurtz and his own decision to elevate him to the rank of moral victor. Both are essentially self-protective gestures designed to defend against some disquieting outcome—either the company's endangered fortunes or Marlow's defeat by the darkness. Marlow implicitly conveys his recognition that Kurtz will serve equally well as a scapegoat whether he is admired or disdained when, in the course of arguing for Kurtz's greatness, he mixes his moral epithets: "the gift of expression, the bewildering, the illuminating, the most exalted and the most contemptible, the pulsating stream of light, or the deceitful flow from the heart of an impenetrable darkness" (79). Whether, as in the eyes of the company, Kurtz is contemptible, or, as seen by the natives, largely exalted, does not in the least affect his efficacy as an outsider around whom Marlow can construct a personal mythology. Likewise, the pilgrims who "buried something [Kurtz's corpse] in a muddy hole" (112) are little different from the Marlow who affirms that Kurtz was a "remarkable man" (120). Both are satisfying a deep, perhaps even an ineradicable, psychological need by establishing a distance between themselves and the man whom they have both agreed to designate as radically unlike themselves.

Marlow fails, however, to perceive the similarity that links him with the other company employees. When speaking of his fellow Europeans he often stresses, on the contrary, the enmity that exists between them. After disagreeing with the manager about Kurtz, for example, he feels that he has been ostracized: "I found myself lumped along with Kurtz as a partisan of methods for which the time was not ripe" (101). Later, he will feel that the disfavor from which he suffers emanates from the company as a whole: "The pilgrims looked upon me with disfavour. I was, so to speak, numbered with the dead" (109–10). Marlow is undoubtedly right in believing that he has become the target of an exclusionary mechanism. This should not, however, obscure the countervailing fact that, despite their apparent differences, Marlow and the company employees are united in their belief that the "remarkable" Kurtz can be made to serve a useful purpose. While they may be at odds about everything else, they do nonetheless agree that Kurtz is deserving of their special and, in fact, their exclusive attention. Marlow points to this underlying bond again when he asserts that Kurtz "wasn't common," an affirmation with which the company manager would surely have agreed.

Unlike Marlow and the pilgrims, however, the underlying structure of the novel itself demystifies the process through which human communities designate their scapegoats. Marlow's esteem for Kurtz is shown to be the expression of a need that tells us nothing useful or reliable about Kurtz himself; rather, it merely shows that, like the blank spaces that Marlow used to "dream gloriously over" (22), he has been called upon to respond to Marlow's psychological needs. Conrad also shows this process at work in the manager's attitude toward Kurtz. We remember that this manager wants to dispose of Kurtz because of the latter's "unsound methods." However, even the most superficial reading of *Heart of Darkness* will lead to the conclusion that Kurtz's methods are not really different in kind from those of the other members of the company. He is set apart from them, not so much by his unexampled depravity, as by their need to believe that the crisis that the company currently faces can be remedied by his expulsion. Conrad has supplied us with ample evidence, however, that "unsound methods" will not disappear with the demise of Kurtz, since he is by no means their only perpetrator. Nor will the immediate prospects of the company be improved by his death, as the manager himself is well aware: "The district is closed to us for a time. Deplorable! Upon the whole, the trade will suffer" (101). We may even surmise that other Europeans will come along to gratify their lusts in such a way as to compromise whatever putative benefits may follow upon Kurtz's exclusion from the company.

Conrad leaves us finally with the suspicion that both Marlow and the company are involved in an activity that, while as old as human history itself, is nonetheless founded upon an illusion. The two opposing stories that are told about Kurtz—as the proponent of "unsound methods" and as the agent of a "moral victory"—are equally based upon a mystification that posits him as "remarkable," thus overlooking his resemblance to those who would set him apart from the crowd and expect from him benefits that he cannot realistically deliver. *Heart of Darkness* subjects belief in Kurtz's difference from the rest of humanity to ironic scrutiny; in this way, it reveals that he is too much like the rest of humanity to sustain the salvific role that Marlow has chosen for him.

The underlying scapegoating mechanism that we find in *Heart of Darkness* points us to a conclusion about Conrad's novel closely resembling that of Ian Watt, who argued that the final meaning of *Heart of Darkness* is not to be found in the meeting between Marlow and Kurtz, but in the implicit reenactment of this meeting aboard the *Nellie,* an occasion that allows Marlow to form a bond with the assembled members of the group by sharing his experience with them. For Watt, *Heart of Darkness* recounts the adventure

> of a man who stumbled into the underworld many years ago, and lived to tell its secrets, although not until much later. Then, mysteriously, the right occasion presented itself: a time and a place that supply both the evocative atmosphere, and the stimulus of an audience with whom Marlow has enough identity of language and experience to encourage him to come to terms at last with some of his most urgent and unappeased moral perplexities through the act of sharing them. (*Conrad in the Nineteenth Century,* 253).

The meeting between Marlow and the men aboard the *Nellie* replays Kurtz's relationships with the natives and the members of the company; in each case a group acquires its sense of solidarity by designating one of its members as an outsider. The meeting aboard the *Nellie,* however, amounts to a sublimated or demystified reenactment of this pattern, one from which all magical and sacrificial elements have been removed.

In foregrounding the bond between Marlow and his listeners, the frame tale suggests, in effect, the possibility of a relationship between a group and its designated outsider that does not lead either to deification or to violent expulsion. The narrator will, to be sure, separate Marlow from the other men who are aboard the *Nellie* by, for example, giving him a surname while attributing only titles (Lawyer, Director, and Accountant) to the others. The recounting of Marlow's journey further calls attention to the distinction between

Marlow, as sole speaker, and the assembled group of his silent listeners: a motif that Marlow himself will underline in his celebrated declaration, "Of course in this you fellows see more than I could then. You see me, whom you know . . . "(50).

The narrator will add even deeper significance to this pattern and, in the process, connect Marlow directly with Kurtz, when he refers to him as "an idol." However, we recognize in this designation an innocent metaphor, which, although invoking supernatural overtones, does not involve any hint of the "unspeakable rites" that accompany Kurtz's elevation in the eyes of the natives or his denigration in the eyes of the company. Similarly, the narrator will lament Marlow's not representing his class without suggesting that this defect should make him the object of some exclusionary ritual. The worst eventuality that awaits Marlow aboard the *Nellie* is that, in telling his story, he will become, especially in the eyes of his subsequent readers, the "non-sacrificial victim" of the numerous ironies to which Conrad subjects him. *Heart of Darkness* implicitly confronts us with the ethical challenge of recognizing Marlow's fallibility without making of him a scapegoat upon whom we discharge the burden of our own susceptibility to delusive constructions of reality.

F. R. Leavis had, in *The Great Tradition*, famously echoed the unnamed narrator's negative judgment of Marlow as a storyteller in his own complaint against the "adjectival insistence" to which he thought Conrad was unfortunately prone. Lapsing into a prosecutorial metaphor, Leavis concluded that

> Conrad must stand here convicted of borrowing the arts of the magazine-writer (who has borrowed his, shall we say, from Kipling and Poe) in order to impose on his readers and on himself, for thrilled response, a "significance" that is merely emotional insistence on the presence of what he can't produce. The insistence betrays the absence, the willed "intensity" the nullity. He is intent on making a virtue out of not knowing what he means. (180)

The tendency of Conrad's prose style that Leavis censures, and which becomes especially pronounced when Kurtz is its object, may, however, be as likely to arouse our suspicions as it is to induce the "hypnotic stupor" that concerned Achebe. The rhetoric both of deification and of disparagement loses its secure moorings and falls into disrepute as it is articulated by Marlow's faltering epithets. Marlow's language, particularly at those moments where the scapegoating mechanism is operating most intensely, leads us to suspect that it designates only a constructed, and not a real, object.

Perry Meisel and Tzvetan Todorov seem to have grasped this point more clearly than Leavis. Meisel, for example, alludes to the demystification of the kernel formed by the outsider that *Heart of Darkness* achieves when he argues that the novella itself counters Marlow's belief that he has discovered the central core of Kurtz by implying that this core simply does not exist: "The 'matter' of Kurtz's meaning escapes Marlow not because this wishful essence is difficult to locate, or as the psychological critics might argue, because it must remain repressed, but because it simply does not exist. . . . There is no central thread in the evidences that constitute his character, much less no deep center to his existence as a surface of signs" ("De-centering," 25). Similarly, Tzvetan Todorov has pointed to the tendency of the narrative techniques of *Heart of Darkness* to efface the isolatable object, whether in the form of a person or of an idea. Kurtz, for example, who is the principal object of knowledge, fails to achieve a definitive form; we want to know who Kurtz is, "but we discover little more than the fact that there is something to discover" ("Knowledge in the Void," 167). Like Meisel, Todorov concludes that "the center does not exist any more than does ultimate meaning" (167). Applying these observations to our own concern with scapegoating, we may observe that this now ungraspable center had heretofore been occupied by a vulnerable and *all-too-graspable* designated victim. The elusive, indeterminate meaning of Marlow's story may be thus interpreted as envisioning a community that does not require its meanings to be readily locatable "within the shell of a cracked nut" (*Heart of Darkness,* 18).

While vestiges of archaic ways of achieving group solidarity have been marginalized in the relationship between Marlow and his listeners, the potentially redemptive function of the outsider—who has now become a storyteller—nonetheless persists. Conrad himself implies this continuity when he describes creative art as a form of "magic" whose purpose is "the edification of mankind" (*Criticism,* 63) Marlow somewhat sheepishly alludes to his role when he reminds his listeners of the time when "I was loafing about, hindering you fellows in your work and invading your homes, just as though I

had a heavenly mission to civilize you" (21). This self-mocking allusion to his behavior is remarkably close to the unreservedly inspiring
description of the artistic function that Conrad offers in the preface
to *The Nigger of the "Narcissus"*: "To arrest, for the space of a breath,
the hands busy about the work of the earth, and compel men en-
tranced by the sight of distant goals to glance for a moment at the
surrounding vision of form and colour, of sunshine and shadows; to
make them pause for a look, for a sigh, for a smile—such is the aim,
difficult and evanescent, and reserved only for a very few to achieve"
(*Criticism*, 148). Conrad further suggests that the artist is able to fulfill this communal function because all men possess at least a
"minute grain" of that artistic faculty that the artist possesses in a
preeminent way (*Criticism*, 63). Hence, while a residue of the archaic
function traditionally attributed to the idol lingers about the storyteller, what finally matters is his *real proximity* to the community
whose anxieties and self-protective gestures he embodies rather than
the atavistic, sacrificial impulses that his *imagined distance* from it
arouses.

As Peter Brooks has noted, the incompleteness of Marlow's own
understanding of his story requires that it be retold and reinter-
preted by successive generations of readers. This process will be in-
terminable, not, however, because the meaning of his story is elusive
but because we are not yet ready to dispense with our scapegoats.
Chinua Achebe's own powerful reading of the novel requires, symp-
tomatically, that he scapegoat Conrad, whom he condemns as a
"thoroughgoing racist" (in Kimbrough, *Heart of Darkness*, 257), Marlow, whom he credits with nothing more admirable than "bleeding
heart sentiments" (256), and the novel itself, which he characterizes
as "a story in which the very humanity of black people is called in
question" (259).

While Achebe's analysis of Africa as a scapegoated "carrier" for
Western anxieties is both acute and invaluable, it needs ultimately to
be superseded by a future reading that does not replicate the sacrificial mechanism that he rightly denounces. In his concluding remarks about Kenneth Burke's hope for a progressive, yet never
entirely fulfilled, quest for "more benevolent stories" about our inevitable scapegoats, C. Allen Carter points implicitly to the kind of
demystified reading to which *Heart of Darkness* invites us:

Though we cannot break from the circle of words, we can choose our words more carefully. Though we cannot resist telling multidimensional stories, we can tell more benevolent stories. If guilt and a concomitant search for scapegoats, then the need to choose our surrogates more self-consciously. If we have to blame someone, let us start by blaming ourselves for participating so blindly in the scapegoat process; then let us proceed to determine crimes and punishments more humanely and more fairly. (*Kenneth Burke,* 136)

Carter's admonition that we look to our own complicity in scapegoating is salutary. Psychological readings of *Heart of Darkness* have tended to assume that the dark regions of the psyche represented by the journey up the Congo River belong to an isolated individual, whether this be Marlow or Kurtz. This assumption has effectively transformed both men into a *tableau vivant* version of the picture of Dorian Gray that has permitted generations of readers to ignore the darkness that lurks within themselves, not as individuals, but as members of communities that practice "unspeakable rites."

# 3

# Borrowed Desire in
# *The Good Soldier*

Unlike the governess, who adheres unwaveringly to her tendentious interpretation of events at Bly, John Dowell frequently reminds us that he is unable to grasp the larger significance of the story that he has been telling. Thinking of Edward Asburnham, for example, he asks himself whether this "raging stallion" is the masculine ideal, one that he, a mere "eunuch," has woefully failed to emulate. His admission to bafflement on this point exemplifies his characteristic response to such questions: "I don't know. And there is nothing to guide us. And if everything is so nebulous about a matter so elementary as the morals of sex, what is there to guide us in the more subtle morality of all other personal contacts, associations, and activities? Or are we meant to act on impulse alone? It is all a darkness" (14).

Toward the end of *The Good Soldier*, however, Dowell claims to have found this meaning in the predilection of "normal" communities for protecting themselves from the abnormal by resorting to ritual expulsion. In the course of developing this insight, he characterizes the events of his story as culminating in "the extinction of two very splendid personalities," Edward and Nancy Rufford, whose punishment allows other people to enjoy "a quiet, comfortable, good time" (253). He then reiterates this interpretation in his claim that Edward and Nancy had to be "sacrificed" so that Leonora could be set up in her "modern mansion" (273). He further believes that the fate of his "splendid personalities" points to a universal communal practice: "Conventions and traditions I suppose work blindly but surely for the preservation of the normal type; for the extinction of proud, resolute, and unusual individuals" (258–59).

Dowell will emphasize the primitive cruelty underlying modern enactments of this practice when he describes Leonora and Nancy Rufford as having "flayed the skin off him [Edward] as if they had done it with whips" and when he characterizes them as "a couple of Sioux who had got hold of an Apache and had him well tied to a stake" (260). Although Edward actually slits his own throat, Dowell attempts, in his description of his death, to stage it as though it were a public execution. As Dowell reminds us, Edward is, after all, a descendant of "the Ashburnham who accompanied Charles I to the scaffold" (7). These various allusions serve to construct an *imagined* scene of ritual violence comparable to the "holocaust" that Nick Carraway will later create for Gatsby.

Denis Donoghue, accepting Dowell's interpretation as the "major judgment of the book," concludes that, in *The Good Soldier,* tragic fate "becomes a neo-Darwinian mutation by which vivid organisms are suppressed so that ordinary, normal, prudent organisms may survive" (Stang, *Presence of Ford Madox Ford,* 52). Associating Edward with the Byronic hero, Donoghue remarks that the emotional effect of the novel depends upon our ambivalence toward the romantic energies that he represents: "The pathos of the book is that the passion to which Dowell appeals has no continuing place in the world. In many senses we have approved its loss; in a residual sense, our approval is itself compromised. We do not want Byronism back, but we cannot be sanguine about the ease with which we have repudiated all such desires" (54). Dowell expresses precisely this ambivalence when, after suggesting that he probably would have found some way of uniting Edward and Florence if they had been drawn to each other by a genuine passion, he confesses: "I do not know where the public morality of the case comes in, and, of course, no man really knows what he would have done in any given case" (100).

Dowell's analysis of the putative meaning of his story is, however, seriously at odds with the actual facts. It involves both the spurious elevation of Edward Ashburnham as a tragic hero and the attribution to his community of vengeful instincts that seem actually to be in abeyance. Dowell comes closer to describing the true nature of this plot when—neglecting to romanticize the solitary figure of Edward as the suffering victim of a hypocritical society—he observes that the society in which he lives is actually characterized by the *declining* authority of its interdictions. Leonora's family, for example, does not require as a condition of her marriage to Edward that their children be raised as Catholics. Leonora, in her turn, rather than acting the part of the offended, censorious wife, actually encourages Edward's adulterous relationships, even to the extent of encouraging Nancy Rufford to offer herself to him sexually. At the time of the Kilsyte affair, Edward benefits, in a related way, from the "ready sympathy"(53) of the judge who tries his case. Even more significantly, his final tragedy is provoked—not by persecution at the hands of a vengeful and unfeeling community—but, as his relationship with Nancy demonstrates, by a collapse of prohibitions that exposes him to the inherent destructiveness of his desire. His subsequent suicide will give Edward what he has sought all along: the encounter with an adversary whose terms—unlike those of his community—are genuinely nonnegotiable.

Unlike "society," whose cruelty he largely imagines, Dowell himself can be quite ruthless in his condemnation of the various villains that he would make into the scapegoats of his story. Somewhat like Marlow aboard the *Nellie*, he tries to create a bond with the "sympathetic soul" whom he imagines as his listener and, who, presumably, can be counted upon to share Dowell's various antipathies, especially toward Florence and (later) Leonora, but also toward Nancy Rufford and Roman Catholicism. He indicts Florence for pursuing "poor dear Edward from vanity" (76) and for causing Leonora's "mental deterioration" (209), and he repeatedly blames Leonora for Edward's successive mishaps. Her Catholicism, furthermore, serves as an "alien" trait that Dowell counts on to bring himself closer to his listener: "In that silent watching, again, I think that she was a Catholic—of a people that can think thoughts alien to ours and keep them to themselves" (144). Nancy will, in her turn, be accused of cruelty in her behavior toward Edward. Dowell's effort to impose a form on his narrative by constructing certain characters as scapegoats does not, however, survive examination. The distinction that he wants to maintain between a "good" Edward, with himself as his chief defendant, and a cohort of "evil" women—including Leonora, Florence and Nancy—is merely a sign of his wishfulness. The fact that Dowell is, even on the most lenient interpretation of his behav-

ior in the novel's concluding scene, an accomplice to Edward's suicide is sufficient evidence to invalidate this simplistic paradigm.

Dowell may be compared to the doctors who had always believed
that the poor health of Florence's Uncle John could be blamed on
his heart. Following his death, they performed (rather implausibly
in the case of an eighty-four-year-old man with a chronic condition)
an autopsy that revealed his lungs, and not his heart, to be at the
root of the problem. The figurative autopsy that Dowell performs on
Edward could have uncovered a similar mistake. While Dowell had
believed all along that Edward's tragedy is the fault of repressive societal conventions, he could have realized, upon reflection, that Edward's desire was, by its very nature, destructive. Edward is possessed
by a desire that forces him, with a rigorous and implacable insistence, to pursue only what he cannot have. In the absence of some
contravening force—in the form, for example, of a societal taboo—
this liberated desire freely drives him to his suicide. Dowell points repeatedly to this source of Edward's destruction when, toward the
end of his narrative, he describes him as "dying for love" (247). He
never quite sees, however, that this is literally true. Dying for love is,
on Dowell's lips, a romantic cliché whose tragic applicability to Edward's situation never comes clearly into view even in the more lucid
moments of Dowell's postmortem.

The work of Uncle Hurlbird's doctors at the time of the autopsy
must, for this reason, be performed by Dowell's "sympathetic listener," who, refusing to be gulled by the romantic illusions that Dowell's misdiagnosis is intent upon preserving, will locate the "lungs"
that produced Edward's fate, not in societal restraints upon his desire, but in the nature of this desire itself. Edward, like the other
major characters of the novel, will only be satisfied if he is allowed, as
it were, to step through the looking glass and become someone
other than himself. The obstacle that he faces is to be located, not in
societal repression—which could, in principle, be lifted—but in the
nature of reality itself. In a related way, Dowell consistently misiden-
tifies the obstacle that Edward pursues in his relationship with Nancy
as "adultery," although "incest" is clearly the more appropriate term.
More broadly, he persistently fails to discover, concealed behind Edward's merely apparent pursuit of the *forbidden,* his genuinely tragic
desire for the *impossible.*

Dowell's hesitation between competing diagnoses of Edward's malaise, as well as his readiness to embrace the less persuasive of them, is amusingly echoed in Uncle John's case by the unwillingness of his surviving relatives to accept the implications of his doctors' discovery (215–17). Believing that he suffered from a heart ailment, Uncle John had left the greater part of his considerable fortune to medical research on this organ. Following the autopsy, however, his relatives decided that it would be more in keeping with the spirit of his will to donate this money to research on lungs. Ford deftly creates a tantalizing symmetry between Edward and Uncle John by making Dowell the executor of the latter's estate. While we never learn how the competing claims of lungs versus heart are resolved, we do know that, facing a similar ambiguity in his diagnosis of Edward, Dowell unhesitatingly chose the more emotionally satisfying of the two alternatives that presented themselves.

The diagnosis of Edward's suffering in *The Good Soldier* follows a path that was already observable in *Heart of Darkness*. In the earlier novel, Marlow encountered savagery twice: in the "grove of death" and in the "unspeakable rites." Guided by comprehensible cultural prejudices, though with a noticeable lack of logical rigor, he decides that cannibalism is unspeakably more horrendous than the callous brutality of the European colonial enterprise. Dowell faces a similar choice: either he can locate the source of Edward's destruction in his self-chosen "race with death" in pursuit of Nancy (128) or in societal taboos. While all of the evidence points to the former of these hypotheses as the more likely, Dowell predictably chooses the latter. Uncle Hurlbird's doctors presumably did not bear any professional responsibility for the misdiagnosis of his illness, which was reasonable but, finally, mistaken. They were not, in any event, guilty of wanting to blame his heart in place of his lungs. Dowell, on the other hand, does bear responsibility for his misdiagnosis of Edward's calamity in the sense that it results from his tendentious readiness to place blame clearly where it does *not* belong, whether with Florence, Leonora, Nancy Rufford or, ultimately, with "society" itself. Added to these, we may note again his unwillingness to confront his own indirect responsibility for Edward's death.

Dowell himself significantly undermines his paradigm of normal community versus abnormal outsider when, precisely at the moment that he is trying to indict society for having persecuted an exceptional individual, he alludes to the fact that the lives of *all* of his characters have resulted in a tragic outcome:

> Leonora wanted Edward, and she got Rodney Bayham, a pleasant enough sort of sheep. Florence wanted Branshaw, and it is I who have bought it from Leonora. I didn't really want it; what I wanted mostly was to cease being a nurse-attendant. Well, I am a nurse attendant. Edward wanted Nancy Rufford and I have got her. Only she is mad. It is a queer and fantastic world. Why can't people have what they want? The things were all there to content everybody; yet everybody has the wrong thing. (257–58)

In this alternative reading of his story's pattern, the mythic image of a community that assures its unity by resorting to the ritual expulsion of a scapegoat gives way to the more accurate portrayal of an entire community of individuals who, each in his or her turn, experiences the tragic outcome that was supposed to be reserved exclusively for its sacrificial victim. Adopting the religious metaphors to which Dowell resorts at key points in his narrative, we may say that, not just Edward, but all of the major characters in *The Good Soldier*, having been expelled from the terrestrial paradise, are consigned to a hell in which they are allowed to have only what they cannot desire.

Dowell's own failure to understand the reasons underlying an outcome that is common to all of his major characters follows from his mistaken belief that the salient feature of their suffering is their inability to *have* some desired object that has unjustly been withheld from them. Upon reflection, however, we discover that their real longing—which cannot be satisfied merely by the possession of desirable objects—is, impossibly, to *become* some desired person by appropriating his or her identity.[1] The Dowells are Americans who want to be British. Edward is a Tory who wants to be a feudal lord. Leonora and Nancy want, forgetting that they live in a modern secularized world, to be Catholic saints. Every character is destroyed by the desire for a life that cannot be theirs because it belongs already to another person or to another historical period. In a variant of this pattern, they will be brought to a tragic end because they want, at one and the same time, to occupy two mutually exclusive positions.

Thus, Edward wants to be both the father and the lover of certain of his women, Nancy wants (or, more precisely, is *made* to want by Leonora) to be both Edward's daughter and his mistress. Leonora wants to be both a model Catholic wife who "succeeded in retaining the fidelity of her husband" (205) and the procurer who facilitates Edward's affairs.

As the numerous allusions to literary works remind us throughout *The Good Soldier,* the desire to be another person may be fulfilled vicariously. Edward can " pass hours reading one of Scott's novels or the Chronicles of Froissart" (151) or indulge his fantasy of being "looked upon as a sort of Lohengrin" (172). Florence, in the midst of a passionate embrace, can be reminded of romantic novels. Dowell can not only write a novel but, going a step further, imagine that he is telling a story in a setting that is itself borrowed from the realm of fiction:

> So I shall just imagine myself for a fortnight or so at one side of the fireplace of a country cottage, with a sympathetic soul opposite me. And I shall go on talking, in a low voice while the sea sounds in the distance and overhead the great black flood of wind polishes the bright stars. From time to time we shall get up and go to the door and look out at the great moon and say: 'Why, it is nearly as bright as in Provence!' And then we shall come back to the fireside, with just the touch of a sigh because we are not in Provence where even the saddest stories are gay. (15)

The tragic movement of the novel is set in motion when characters, setting their reading aside, attempt in real life to cross the boundary that marks the division between themselves and another person. In trying to step through the looking glass in which they see the reflected images of their idols, they collide with an obdurate reality that returns them to their actual selves, which have been made even ghostlier by their impossible quest. Florence is shown to be merely a pale copy of Leonora, while Edward makes "pretty speeches out of books that he had read" (153). Nancy imperfectly parrots the opening lines of the Catholic *Credo,* and Dowell becomes the dithering memorialist of the man who cuckolded him. This predicament is faced—not in exalted isolation by Edward Ashburnham—but by all of the major characters.

Dowell persistently obfuscates the generic quality of Edward's suffering, however, by resorting to grandiloquent metaphors. Thus he
will speculate that Edward alone has been "tormented by blind and
inscrutable destiny," which, a moment later, he will rename "inscrutable and blind justice" (54). Dowell's subsequent allusion to
"the tempestuous forces that pushed that miserable fellow on to
ruin" (56) further contributes to the effect of rhetorical inflation
that obscures the simple fact that Edward, like the other protagonists
in the novel, has become trapped by the double bind that results
when a forbidden object becomes somewhat less-than-forbidden. At
that moment, the conflicts that are no longer kept at bay by respect
for interdictions reappear in forms whose "tempestuousness" can be
readily and satisfactorily understood without resort to Dowell's deceptive metaphors. Edward suffers as he does because he can only
desire a woman who belongs in some way to another man, whether
real or virtual. It is not so much the woman herself as the illusory opportunity to *be* the man for whom she is destined that leads him onward to the ultimate catastrophe of his quasi-incestuous relationship
with Nancy Rufford. Far from being a rebel against social conventions, such as Dowell would like to portray him, Edward depends on
them to indicate desirable women to him. This reliance on convention to stimulate desire seems already to have been at work in his relatively innocent decision to marry Leonora even though—or especially because—he was expected to ask for the hand of the eldest
Powys daughter.

Since Dowell does not explain Edward's choice in terms of
Leonora's personal qualities, it is reasonable to conclude that he was
guided by an impersonal desire to reject the daughter who was made
for him by social convention and to marry the one who was intended, according to the same convention, for another man. The
trap into which he falls here does not become entirely apparent
until the arrival of Nancy Rufford. The intense passion that Nancy
arouses in Edward, as well as the intolerable suffering to which this
leads, is entirely produced by the prohibition against incest.[2]

The sexual possession that Nancy offers to Edward (with ardent,
if improbable, coaching from Leonora) is not, however, the forbidden contact with a "redeeming woman" that Dowell imagines it to
be. As Edward's refusal of Nancy implicitly acknowledges, his possessing her would, rather, have proved irrefutably that no merely for-

bidden goal can satisfy the truly impossible desire that possesses Edward. Dowell would like us to believe that, if only Edward had been allowed to unite with an "ultimately satisfying woman," he would not have killed himself: the frustrated desire for this woman led him to despair and, thence, to his death, according to Dowell's misdiagnosis. In fact, however, it matters little whether Edward had possessed Nancy or not, since what draws him to her is not the "girl" herself, but the impossibility that she represents. When she does actually offer herself to him, he is forced to refuse her so that she will remain inaccessible to him.

The pattern whereby desire, in the absence of a contravening restraint, predictably seeks, not fulfillment, but an invincible obstacle, likewise applies in general to relationships between American and British characters. Florence, for example, begins innocently enough as an anglophile American whose dreams lead to tragedy because she cannot resist the temptation to overstep an unbridgeable boundary by actually *becoming* the real British lady that Leonora already is. Florence was herself already halfway to being British, since her ancestors had owned property near Edward Ashburnham's family's estate for several centuries. More recently, the Hurlbird family from which she is descended was on the side of the British during the revolutionary war. Florence wished, however, to take her proto-Britishness a step further: "She wanted to marry a gentleman of leisure; she wanted a European establishment. She wanted her husband to have an English accent, an income of fifty thousand dollars a year from real estate and no ambitions to increase that income" (87).

Her longing for such a gentleman, however, leads her into hopeless competition with a woman who already has one: "It really worried poor Florence that she couldn't, in matters of culture, ever get the better of Leonora. I don't know what Leonora knew or what she didn't know but certainly she was always there whenever Florence brought out any information" (44). Dowell alludes again to the pathos of Florence's being trapped by this rivalistic compulsion with her English model when he observes her doing her "homework" before one of their cultural outings. As he clearly recognizes (with a clarity of vision that deserts him, however, when he turns his attention to Edward), the pursuit of this dream depersonalizes her: "I thought suddenly that she wasn't real; she was just a mass of talk out of guidebooks, of drawings out of fashion-plates. It is even possible that if that feeling had not possessed me, I should have run up sooner to her room and might have prevented her drinking the prussic acid. But I just couldn't do it; it would have been like chasing a scrap of paper—an occupation ignoble for a grown man" (134).

Dowell himself seems likewise to become the comical victim of his desire to have his value certified in the eyes of the British. We notice this, for example, in his feelings about the letters that he addresses to the editors of newspapers: "I have written . . . letters to the *Times* that the *Times* never printed; those that I wrote to the Paris edition of the New York *Herald* were always printed, but they never seemed to satisfy me when I saw them" (51). The double bind into which Dowell's desire for recognition has thrust him—whereby idealized British editors, who alone are capable of conferring the only distinction that he desires, choose to withhold it—also appears in his speculation that, in Leonora's eyes, he and Florence are nothing more than "two casual Yankees whom she could not have regarded as being much more than a carpet beneath her feet" (57). Dowell's inevitable exclusion from the only club to which he would like to belong is ironically underlined by his ignorance as to whether or not a farewell "God bless you" as he takes leave of Edward would be approved by the social code whose exclusive custodians are the members of Edward and Leonora's social class.

The predicament to which Dowell alludes here is a paradigm of the novel as a whole, which points unfailingly to the inextricable connection between the desirability of an object and its inaccessibility. Thus, the distant view of the cliffs of England as seen from Calais is as close as Florence will ever come to fulfilling her dream of being received by English society. Even if the obstacle created by her "heart" could be resolved, she would still find that the conventions that have created so ultimately desirable an object as English country life also guarantee that she will never enter into it: "She would make him [Edward] kiss her at any moment of the day; and it was only by his making it plain that a divorced lady could never assume a position in the country of Hampshire that he could prevent her from making a bolt of it with him in her train" (108). Dowell returns to this double bind a moment later when he mentions that Florence is prevented from divorcing him by her recognition that "[i]t would have meant the extinction of all hopes of Branshaw Manor for her" (109).

While Dowell is intent upon asserting Edward's exceptional-
ness—and, above all, his complete unlikeness to Florence—Edward's behavior follows a path that had already been traveled by his
mistress. Like Florence, he is caught in a double bind that obliges
him to pass through a succession of women who have been made
only relatively inaccessible by social convention until he finds, in
Nancy Rufford, the woman with whom he will undertake the final
race toward the death that he has always sought vainly in the company of her predecessors. Dowell laments the fact that Edward's pursuit of emotional fulfillment is repeatedly frustrated by the presence
of some obstacle: "But there was always an obstacle—if the lady were
married there would be a husband who claimed the greater part of
her time and attention. If, on the other hand, it were an unmarried
girl he could not see very much of her for fear of compromising her"
(172). Dowell's regret for Edward's misfortune, however, never once
leads him to ponder the possibility that this obstacle, far from being
an extraneous and accidental accompaniment to Edward's desire,
may actually have been its intended object. He romanticizes Edward's behavior as motivated by his "mad passion to find an ultimately satisfying woman" (55). More careful analysis of Edward's
successive adventures reveals, however, that the desired object is not
so much the woman herself as it is the "ultimately satisfying" frustration that she provokes.

Dowell points to Edward's habit of desiring what already belongs
to another person (and, implicitly, to the possibility that the other
person will in some way oppose this appropriation) when he refers
to him as "a raging stallion neighing after his neighbors' womenkind" (14). Similarly, he continually stresses, in his description of
each of Edward's women, the fact of their belonging to another
man. His habit of marginalizing chronology throughout his narrative obscures, however, the increasingly endogamic, if not incestuous, character of Edward's affairs. La Dolciquita, the first of Edward's women, is simply a "cosmopolitan harpy who passed for the
mistress of a Russian Grand Duke" (60). His next affair, however, is
with a woman whom Dowell describes as "the wife of a brother officer" (63), an emphasis that brings us somewhat closer to the incestuous desire that will draw Edward irresistibly to Nancy. The presence of a male rival is even more strongly pronounced in Dowell's
giving priority to the *spouse* when he introduces Edward's next mis-

tress—"Major Basil, the husband of the lady who next, and really, comforted the unfortunate Edward" (180). Edward then repeats this pattern in his pursuit of Dowell's wife Florence who, while apparently Leonora's inferior in every conceivable way, is made irresistible by her belonging to Dowell, who regards Edward as "a large elder brother" (275). His compulsive adulteries suggest that what he really wants is not an "ultimately satisfying woman," but the encounter with an adversary capable of successfully contesting his claim to her. Following his principle of blaming the "heart" rather than the "lungs," however, Dowell will consistently ascribe the threats to Edward's well-being as though they were visited upon him by everyone but himself.

Like Edward, Dowell will dutifully pursue an object of desire only on condition that it also become an obstacle. Edward is brought to his tragic end by his quest for a genuinely inaccessible woman. Dowell, in his turn, experiences a characteristically pathetic destiny that is similarly brought about by women who are not available to him. First, there is Florence, whose "illness," as Dowell himself recognizes, makes of her "at once a wife and an unattainable mistress" (53). Much later, he will find himself reliving this seemingly unalterable pattern when his desire to emulate Edward Ashburnham leads him to desire marriage with Nancy Rufford, which is prohibited this time—not by the taboo against incest—but by the impediment of insanity.

The motif of the looking glass through which the major characters in *The Good Soldier* would like to pass is, as was mentioned earlier, pervasively echoed by the numerous literary borrowings that permeate the novel. Dowell, for example, likens Edward to Odysseus when, alluding to his affair with La Dolciquita, he describes him as being "in the arms of his Circe" (61). Edward thinks of himself as the new Lohengrin while, for Nancy Rufford, "He was the Cid; he was Lohengrin; he was the Chevalier Bayard" (246). Dowell will likewise use literary metaphors to underline this derivative element, as when, in the midst of recounting Edward's moonlight encounter with Nancy, he exclaims, "[i]t is melodrama; but I can't help it" (123), and when he alludes somewhat dismissively to Florence as wishing "to appear like a heroine of a French comedy" (131). Toward the end of *The Good Soldier,* Dowell will enlist a literary allusion in his effort to imbue Edward with heroic grandeur: "I seem to see poor Edward, naked

and reclining amidst darkness, upon cold rocks, like one of the ancient Greek damned, in Tartarus, or wherever it was" (274).

These explicit literary echoes all tend, in keeping with the exaltation that Dowell intends for Edward, to romanticize his predicament. Ford, however, weaves into the novel many details that point
to Dante's *Divine Comedy* as an *implicit* subtext that, rather than echo-
ing Dowell's delusive portrayal of Edward, radically demystifies it.
While Dante is never mentioned by name, Dowell does allude to the
three phases of the *Divine Comedy*, when he mentions heaven, hell,
and what he calls the "intermediate stage" (which he mistakenly
identifies as limbo). Likewise, Dante cannot be far from his mind (or
from Ford's) when he wonders, "Is there any terrestrial paradise
where, amidst the whispering of the olive-leaves, people can be with
whom they like and have what they like and take their ease in shadows and in coolness" (258).

For Dowell, the Catholic Church itself is largely a curious and
perhaps perverse, though rather harmless, presence in modern-day
England. He does, however, allow at one point that this church may
be no stranger than the human beings entrusted to its care: "perhaps Roman Catholics, with their queer, shifty ways, are always right.
They are dealing with the queer, shifty thing that is human nature"
(269). Of the numerous examples of human shiftiness that Dante
presents in the *Divine Comedy* the most relevant to an understanding
of *The Good Soldier* is the story of Paolo and Francesca in canto 5 of
the *Inferno*. The canto itself concerns the fate of adulterers who—
much like the Nancy Rufford's "shuttlecocks"—are buffeted about
by the winds of their chaotic passions. The story of tragic love that
Francesca recounts to Dante has, in particular, two aspects that are
of special relevance to *The Good Soldier*. In the first place, Francesca
romanticizes the nature of the passion that drew her to Paolo, which
she attributes to the spontaneous workings of "love," much as Dowell
will romanticize Edward's apparently spontaneous longing for union
with the "ultimately satisfying woman."

Dante captures the poignancy of Francesca's misunderstanding
on this point by having her allude repeatedly to the love that she believes to have been the cause of her ruin. In response to Dante's request for further details, however, Francesca offers an account that
radically revises her initial story. While it was love that guided them
to their doom the first time around, now this role is attributed to a

courtly romance—the medieval equivalent of the sentimental novels of which Edward Ashburnham is so fond:

> One day, to pass the time away, we read
> of Lancelot—how love had overcome him.
> We were alone, and we suspected nothing.
>     And time and time again that reading led
> our eyes to meet, and made our faces pale,
> and yet one point alone defeated us.
>     When we had read how the desired smile
> was kissed by one who was so true a lover,
> this one, who never shall be parted from me,
>     while all his body trembled, kissed my mouth.
>
> (lines 127–36)

This double representation of Paolo and Francesca's adultery—as the consequence of a spontaneous passion and of a borrowed desire that will eventually provoke rivalry (with Francesca's husband, Gianciotto Malatesta, who also happens to be Paolo's older brother)—operates, much more obscurely to be sure, but just as centrally in *The Good Soldier*. Ford's novel is essentially the story of a group of people who—thinking that they were acting upon their deepest and most passionate impulses—were actually responding obediently to cues that had been given to them by a depersonalizing passion.[3]

Dowell and Edward, for their part, correspond to the two quite different faces of Paolo that Dante shows us: first, as Francesca's romantic lover and, second, as the pathetic figure that Dante meets in the *Inferno*. The first Paolo, who resembles Edward, takes hold of Francesca "through his beauty" (104). The Paolo that Dante shows us in hell, however, is a drastically degraded version of the romantic figure described by Francesca. Completely overshadowed by Francesca, who alone talks to Dante, Paolo reminds us in his enfeeblement more of Dowell than of Edward. His only contribution to the story of their romance is the tears that he weeps throughout Francesca's narrative.

Whether or not Ford had this celebrated episode from the *Inferno* in mind as he wrote *The Good Soldier*, he has intuitively borrowed for his novel Dante's stark contrast between the apparent spontaneity and naturalness of desire and its contrived, imitative, and ultimately destructive reality. Francesca's revelation that the passion that consumed herself and Paolo had been plagiarized from a book that they had been reading recalls Dowell's allusions to Edward's fondness for sentimental novels from which he borrows his ideas about love: "And yet I must add that poor dear Edward was a great reader—he would pass hours lost in novels of a sentimental type—novels in which type-writer girls married marquises and governesses earls. And in his books, as a rule, the course of true love ran as smooth as buttered honey" (30).[4] Also like Dante, who shows us two radically distinct versions of Paolo, Ford explores the experience of borrowed desire through two radically dissimilar characters. He uses Edward to exemplify the passions that, however duplicitous, appeal powerfully to the romantic imagination. The borrowed quality of these desires, while frequently alluded to, will be eclipsed by Edward's vibrant and adventurous personality. Dowell, for his part, then shows us, without any mitigating attractiveness, the pathetic face of these same desires.

Dowell recognizes the profound affinity between himself and Edward when he admits that he loved "him because he was just myself. If I had had the courage and the virility and possibly also the physique of Edward Ashburnham I should, I fancy, have done much what he did" (275). The irony here is that, perhaps much more than he realizes, Dowell has, in his own diffident and unappealing way, done precisely what Edward had done before him. Not only has he bought Edward's estate, but he has become the guardian of Nancy Rufford, upon whom he is free to bestow all of the fatherly attentions that had earlier inspired Edward. Of course, Dowell's achievements have none of the romantic aura that had surrounded Edward's adventures. In the *Inferno*, Paolo is reduced to weeping; in *The Good Soldier*, his modern counterpart is given a rambling, feckless narrative through which he arouses our pity rather than our desire to emulate him.

While Dowell, who is the primary reader of the events of the novel, has his gaze admiringly fixed on a "raging stallion," we, as the readers who come after him, are treated to the less tantalizing spectacle of a "eunuch." As Dowell himself admits in a telling remark, he has followed Edward Ashburnham only "faintly" (257). Thus, while Dowell had wanted his story to be about the scapegoating of Edward by an unfeeling community, it proves, finally, to be about his own desire to model himself, in however desultory or cheerless a fashion, upon Edward. For this reason, the crippled figure of Dowell epitomizes—every bit as much as the romantic figure of Edward—the more generalized fate of an *entire community* that is condemned—in the absence of protective restraints—to want only an unattainable object. Dowell is no Edward Ashburnham, but neither is Edward a Lohengrin or a Charles I.

Vincent Cheng has usefully remarked on the mistaken readiness of readers of *The Good Soldier* to assume that Dowell's scorn for Roman Catholicism reflects Ford's own point of view. Cheng points, on the contrary, to "the key role religious issues and affiliations play in so many of the novels, including all of the major ones: *The Good Soldier,* the *Parade's End* tetralogy, and *The Fifth Queen* trilogy ("Spirit of *The Good Soldier,*" 303). He supports this claim by quoting from a letter written to Lucy Masterman at the time Ford was working on *The Good Soldier* and in which he affirms his belief that "clearness of thought" is not possible "unless one either is or has been intensely religious" (Ludwig, *Letters of Ford,* 54). Cheng further emphasizes the importance for Ford of the distinction between "a Protestant English world based on emotional repression" and "a Continental Catholic society based on the instinctual, the sense of divine mystery, and the open expression of feelings" (Cheng, "Spirit of *The Good Soldier,*" 313). He concludes that "the England of Ford's novels acquires the poignant perspective of a race tragically and hypocritically committed to the façade of good form and emotional repression, ignoring the realm and truths of the intuitive and the passionate" (314). In an earlier article on this subject, Cheng had suggested that "[p]erhaps in depicting such a biased and anti-Catholic narrator, Ford in fact wrote a moral tale much more sympathetic toward the Catholic faith than has usually been assumed by focussing on the moral relativism and emptiness of a beleaguered, faithless world exemplified by the tale and its teller" ("Religious Differences in *The Good Soldier,*" 247).

Cheng's suggestion that the novel itself may invite a more favorable evaluation of Catholicism than Dowell's may help us to situate within the context of its larger issues the peculiar "passion" that Edward experiences for the Blessed Mother. Leonora discovers her husband in his bedroom engrossed in the contemplation of a portrait of Virgin Mary:

> Edward was kneeling beside his bed with his head hidden in the counterpane. His arms, outstretched, held out before

him a little image of the blessed virgin—a tawdry, scarlet and Prussian-blue affair that the girl had given him on her first return from the convent. His shoulders heaved convulsively three times, and heavy sobs came from him before she could close the door. He was not a Catholic; but that was the way it took him. (147)

This scene has a curious bearing on Edward's "mad passion to find an ultimately satisfying woman" (55). Dante, of course, finds this woman in Beatrice, who supervises his purification in the earthly paradise and, later, in the Blessed Mother, who will guide him through the celestial paradise to his ultimate meeting with God. The essential difference between Dante and Edward, to be sure, is that the women who are objects of Dante's longing never become merely the instruments for the satisfaction of his passions. By contrast, in *The Good Soldier,* Florence, Leonora, and Nancy Rufford all play the roles assigned to them by a script that has been fashioned by Edward's fantasies. In the desacralized world inhabited by Edward Ashburnham, there is no feminine figure—the equivalent of Beatrice or the Blessed Mother—capable of distancing herself from those who desire her. The foundational Catholic figure of a woman who is both infinitely desirable and, in a positive way, ultimately inaccessible, whose real, although invisible, existence Dante could take for granted, is simply not available to Edward.

The absence of feminine figures whose inaccessibility transforms them into objects of sublimated longings, creates an essentially claustrophobic, prison-like world in which an alternative to destructive, narcissistic cravings has become inconceivable. This absence— or its merely ironic presence in the figure of Leonora, whom Dowell persistently demonizes—condemns Edward to the compulsive pursuit of ever more elusive objects of desire. Edward's predicament— like that of all of the major characters—is the lack of a protective distance between himself and the objects that solicit his attention. He cannot resist wanting to possess Nancy Rufford sexually, a temptation that Leonora, against all probability, abets. Florence cannot resist wanting to *have* Edward Ashburnham, nor can Dowell resist wanting to *be* him. Each character will, paradoxically, be led to a tragic destiny by the irresistible proximity of an object that fails to remain at a tolerably safe distance.

The situation of the protagonists, characterized as it is by their relation to objects of desire whose "not entirely forbidden" quality provokes intolerable frustration, is curiously replicated by Dowell's
relation to the "saddest story" that he recounts to his silent listener.
Critics of the novel have repeatedly called attention both to the subjectivity of Dowell's narrative and to its apparent lack of intelligibility
without, however, grasping the profound interconnection between
the two. On the one hand, the story seems to have no objective structure—no "master narrative" that commands the manner of its presentation.[5] Dowell is free—to a degree that greatly departs from
traditional norms—to manipulate the materials of his story. His lib-
eration from traditional constraints is especially curious in light of
the fact that he imagines his narrative to be, not a written document,
but an oral narrative recited to a "sympathetic soul" in a country cot-
tage. The form that his narrative eventually takes, however, clearly
makes demands that readers of the novel find highly challenging
and which would undoubtedly have been beyond the capacities of
an actual listener. It is quite impossible to imagine such a listener re-
fraining from the temptation to interrupt Dowell's narration and to
challenge his interpretation of his story. Such a reader would, for example, surely have wondered if the suspiciously long list of major
events that occurred on 4 August—Florence's birth, the beginning
of her journey around the world, the loss of her virginity, her marriage, the beginning of her affair with Edward, and her death—is
based on actual fact or is, rather, a projection of Dowell's need for
some sort of order and clarity on his narrative materials.[6]

Theodore Dreiser famously objected to the narrative technique
of *The Good Soldier*, as opposed to its plot, which he found fascinating:
"It is a sad story, and a splendid one from a psychological point of
view; but Mr. Hueffer, in spite of the care he has bestowed upon it,
has not made it splendid in the telling" (155). Dreiser would have
advised Ford to begin the story with the event that really does set
later events in motion, i.e., with Colonel Powys's decision to marry
off his daughters. While granting that Ford may begin his story
where he likes, Dreiser nevertheless finds him guilty of having ignored a really implacable rule: "Of far more importance is it that,
once begun, it should go forward in a more or less direct line, or at
least that it should retain one's uninterrupted interest. This is not
the case in this book. The interlacings, the cross references, the re-

references to all sorts of things which subsequently are told some-where in full, irritate one to the point of laying down the book" ("Saddest Story," 156).

Frank G. Nigro echoes the view of many defenders of Dowell's narrative style when he argues that "*The Good Soldier* effectively mir-rors what was happening in contemporary art: Ford created a picto-rial, even Cubist novel" ("Who Framed *The Good Soldier*?"382). At the same time, however, Nigro recognizes that Ford was not merely adapting techniques that originated in painting to the novel. Rather, he was also registering his misgivings as to the epistemological im-plications of cubism: "His technique is a political statement in both the narrowest and broadest senses, showing how even indeterminacy can become tyrannical by pictorializing itself as something 'other' than what it is, by throwing a smokescreen over the artist's inten-tions" (383). Nigro detects behind the apparent capriciousness of Dowell's narrative method the intention of deceiving the reader as to his own role in precipitating the tragic events of the novel: "Dow-ell manipulates novelistic techniques and sees through novelistic glasses whenever it proves convenient to his agenda, which is to lead the reader away from any suspicion of his complicity in the round of deaths in *The Good Soldier* and to 'frame' his wife within the novel. Ford gives Dowell the means to frame himself for the reader" (385).

While such hypotheses regarding Dowell's subjective motivations may indeed be valid, they risk obscuring the deeper structural con-nection between the extreme subjectivity of Dowell's narrative style and the tragic implications of the story that it conveys. The readiness of the materials of this story to respond to each of Dowell's passing whims corresponds to the apparent readiness, within the story itself, of objects of desire to be manipulated by the passions of the chief characters. Just as there is no moral code sufficiently powerful to protect characters from their destructive passions, so also there is no narrative code that will mediate Dowell's relation to his listener and, eventually, to his readers. Along these lines, Roger Poole has offered a closely argued defense of his hypothesis that Ford actually in-tended *The Good Soldier* to be read as a parody or simulacrum of the Jamesian or Conradian novel and that, to this end, he consciously deformed the techniques of modernist narration to create an effect of "fauxsemblance." In the course of substantiating his argument, Poole lists the succession of incoherencies in which Dowell indulges—of character, of plot, and of time schemes—that effectively deprive his story of any persuasive claim to verisimilitude.

The story's apparent susceptibility to Dowell's narrative manipulations will ultimately prove, however, to be a fatal trap—the narrative equivalent of the suicidal impasse to which Edward is led by the lure of incest. The story that is so totally available to Dowell is, at the same time, completely inaccessible to him. He can fail to name Nancy Rufford for as long as he wants, withhold his (limited) understanding of events until long after the first mention of the events themselves, and even nearly forget to tell us about the circumstances of Edward's death. These liberties will, however, be persistently accompanied by the admission that he cannot master the significance of his story. The various perspectives to which it willingly submits merely ensure that he will never come within reach of its essential meaning.

The epistemological considerations that are at issue in the narrative style of *The Good Soldier* are doubtlessly important on their own terms. Michael Levenson has suggested, in this regard, that "*The Good Soldier* reveals an incommensurability between life as known and life as experienced, and perhaps the most compelling aspect of its characterization is the flight of personality from the rational categories adduced to explain it" ("Character in *The Good Soldier*," 382). The novel itself, however, loses a considerable part of its moral significance if we regard it largely as a fictional representation of such related subjects as skepticism, moral relativism, and the undecidability of truth. The deeper significance of Ford's choice of Dowell as the narrator of his "saddest story" is that it invites us to ponder the curious combination of intimacy and inaccessibility that characterizes the relationship between his protagonists and their objects of desire. The "incommensurable" gap that Levenson finds between experience and its interpretation indicates the inadequacy of Dowell's interpretive scheme more than the nature of reality itself. Earlier in his article Levenson had defined the "passionate instant" as that which "defies standards of intelligibility, resists the generalities of social explanation, and rests its claim to our attention on one incontrovertible fact: it exists" (377). In fact, however, nothing is more readily intelligible in the novel than the nature of Edward's passion, except to readers who, like Dowell, obscure its origins by constant recourse to the romantic myth of spontaneous desire. Levenson himself avoids falling into this trap by recognizing that passion proves, ultimately, to be more tyrannical than the conventions that it would overturn.

In reflecting on the enduring greatness of *The Good Soldier*, Thomas Moser locates its special excellence in the portrayal of Edward Ashburnham:

> And yet, *The Good Soldier* is great not so much for its bitter tone as for the almost filial love that Dowell feels for Edward (analogous presumably to Ford's deepest feelings for Marwood). If Edward's flaws of stupidity, self-indulgence, and sentimentality lie exposed, they are simply aspects of the great, living human being Ford was determined once in his life to create. Even if we do not believe that Edward, by virtue of his passion, quite belongs with Nancy among the "Beati Immaculati," he is appallingly human in his suffering. (*Life in the Fiction*, 193)

While Moser doubtlessly speaks for countless admirers of *The Good Soldier* my own analysis of the novel leads to the quite different conclusion that Dowell's appealing portrait of Edward depends for its deceptive effect on our readiness to overlook the common fate that he shares with the other characters in the novel. Furthermore, it is not so much Edward himself as it is the *process of displacement* to which Dowell resorts in constructing his portrait that we should be attentive. He succeeds in portraying Edward as "a great, living human being" only because he has transferred criticism of his hero's pathetic, morally repugnant, or merely ludicrous qualities to other characters: himself, to be sure, but also his wife. Curiously, Dowell most closely approaches an accurate portrayal of Edward when he is criticizing Florence for her "sheer vanity" (76).

He deftly captures the essence of the situation that Florence shares with Edward in a powerful metaphor that expresses his wife's futile competition with Leonora:

> Have you ever seen a retriever dashing in play after a greyhound? You see the two running over a green field, almost side by side, and suddenly the retriever makes a friendly snap at the other. And the greyhound simply isn't there. You haven't observed it quicken its speed or strain a limb; but there it is, just

two yards in front of the retriever's outstretched muzzle. So it
was with Florence and Leonora in matters of culture. (44)

He later portrays Edward as similarly engaged in a race that he is
fore-ordained to lose:

> That at any rate was the case with Edward and the poor girl.
> It was quite literally the case that his passions—for the mistress
> of the Grand Duke, for Mrs. Basil, for little Mrs. Maidan, for
> Florence, for whom you will—these passions were merely pre-
> liminary canters compared to his *final race with death for her.* I
> am certain of that. I am not going to be so American as to say
> that all true love demands some sacrifice. It doesn't. But I
> think that love will be truer and more permanent in which
> self-sacrifice has been exacted. (128; my emphasis).

As these metaphors make clear, both Edward and Florence are involved in a race that pits them against an invincible adversary.
Throughout his narrative, however, Dowell obscures this symmetry
by romanticizing Edward's pursuit of women and mocking Florence's failure to compete, successively, with Leonora and Nancy. He
allows Edward to be a "raging stallion forever neighing after his
neighbour's womenkind" (14) while casting Florence in the decidedly less glamorous role of a mere "retriever." Similarly, he will repeatedly diminish his wife in our eyes by constantly calling attention
to the appeal of the "greyhound" with whom she must compete,
without, however, matching Edward against a correspondingly impressive "neighbor," except, perhaps, the occulted figure of death itself.

Dowell will also intimate the factitious, borrowed quality of the
personas that Edward and Florence have fashioned for themselves,
but only in a way that virtually guarantees that we will not spontaneously recognize their resemblance. In a passage from which I
quoted earlier, he observes, dismissively, of Florence, that "she was
just a mass of talk out of guidebooks, of drawings out of fashion-
plates." In contrast, he describes Edward, rather more appealingly, as
"making pretty speeches out of books that he had read" to Leonora
before their marriage and as creating for himself a personality that is
modeled on the heroes of historical or sentimental novels.

The enduring appeal of Ford's masterpiece may ultimately have less to do with any individual character than with the role that its author has bequeathed to the "sympathetic soul" for whom his narrative is intended. Such a reader will, each time that he rereads the novel, share with Ford the joy that he expressed in his dedicatory letter to Stella Ford more than a decade after the publication of *The Good Soldier:* "Great Heavens, did I write as well as that then?" (*Good Soldier,* xxi). Along with the stylistic perfection that Ford achieved in this novel, he has left us a moral riddle, in the form of Edward's spiritual ailment, that we will never entirely solve, not because the solution is not apparent, but because, like Dowell, we are too strongly attached to its misdiagnosis.

# 4

## *The Great Gatsby:*
## Romance or Holocaust?

LIKE MARLOW AND JOHN DOWELL, WHO ARE HIS PRINCIPAL PRECURsors, Nick Carraway invites his readers to contemplate in Jay Gatsby the fate of a man whom he invests with the traits of a hero. In the course of his narrative, he will resort accordingly to strategies whose purpose is to convince us that Gatsby himself is immeasurably superior to the characters who form the backdrop to the story of his dream. As in *Heart of Darkness* and *The Good Soldier,* the tragedy that befalls this hero will be described in terms that have strongly sacrificial overtones. Somewhat like the governess in *The Turn of the Screw,* Nick tends to present his judgments of characters and events in such a way as to preempt rather than to invite alternative interpretations. If, however, we resist the invitation to take his commentary at face value, we will discover that, as was generally true in the earlier novels, the elevation of the protagonist is itself largely spurious and the communal persecution to which he has been subjected is highly conjectural.

In an otherwise appreciative response to Fitzgerald's novel, H. L. Mencken expressed a reservation about the basic story itself, which he characterized as "no more than a glorified anecdote" (Claridge, *F. Scott Fitzgerald,* 156). Fitzgerald, in a letter to Edmund Wilson, speculated that what Mencken did not find in *Gatsby* was "any emotional backbone at the very height of it" (Turnbull, *Letters of Fitzgerald,* 342). Readers of the novel, however, have tended to overlook the self-evident fact that the novel's ostensible emotional center—the reunion between Gatsby and Daisy—does not possess sufficient significance to justify the classic status that has been largely accorded to Fitzgerald's novel. We need only remember Daisy's effusive appreciation of Gatsby's shirts—or the even more telling fact that the truly romantic moments in Daisy and Gatsby's relationship all occurred several years earlier in Louisville and that the period of the reunion is scarcely mentioned in the novel—to convince ourselves that the putative grandeur of Gatsby's dream does not adequately account for the novel's power or its lasting significance.

Reading *Gatsby* as a novel about its hero's dream makes of it the precarious literary achievement whose numerous absurdities were perceptively delineated by the English novelist L. P. Hartley, who, while admiring Fitzgerald's literary gifts, thought that he had squandered them in *Gatsby*. Hartley offered, in a 1926 review of the novel, the following summary of its plot:

> An adventurer of shady antecedents builds a palace at a New York seaside resort, entertains on a scale which Lucullus would have marveled at but could not have approved, and spends untold sums of money, all to catch the eye of his one time sweetheart, who lives on an island opposite, unhappily but very successfully married. At last, after superhuman feats of ostentation and display, the fly walks into the web. A train of disasters follows, comparable in quantity and quality with the scale of the Great Gatsby's prodigies of hospitality. Coincidence leaps to the helm and throws a mistress under a motorcar. The car does not stop, which, all things considered, is the most natural thing that happens in the book. An injured husband finds the Great Gatsby in suicidal mood sitting on a raft in his artificial lake and (apparently) forestalls him; anyhow they are both discovered dead. The elder Gatsby is unearthed and gives a pathetic account of his son's early years. All the characters behave as though they were entitled to grieve over a great sorrow, and the book closes with the airs of tragedy. (Claridge, *F. Scott Fitzgerald*, 178)

Minor inaccuracies aside, this must be among the most cogent and disabused responses that the plot of *The Great Gatsby* has ever received. It is such a welcome antidote to the reams of interpretation of the novel produced by critics who, dutifully aping Nick Carraway in this respect, have allowed their conviction as to Gatsby's greatness to be matched only by their equally adamant certainty as to the moral tawdriness of Tom and Daisy Buchanan. As Hartley's exasperated summary reminds us, *The Great Gatsby*, when read as the account of the eponymous hero's dream and its demise, simply cannot support the weight of morally serious interpretation that it would like to invite or that so many of its critics, in their turn, would like to bestow upon it.[1]

Nor do we move any closer to appreciating the greatness of *Gatsby* by shifting our attention to the growth in moral awareness that countless critics have attributed to Nick Carraway, whose self-evaluation as "one of the few honest people that I have ever known" (64) should in itself arouse our suspicions.[2] As we shall see, the fruits of Nick's presumed moral education amount to little more than a self-serving mystification. Likewise, his inchoate effort to express the significance of his story is far less convincing than the profound insight into the hollowness of Gatsby's romantic dream that he *inadvertently* gives us when making the passing remark that Gatsby loved Daisy because she was the most desirable prize in the eyes of all the other young men of Louisville. This remark allows us to glimpse a truth that Nick perceives only dimly: Gatsby's desire for Daisy was induced in him by the desires of men, such as Tom Buchanan, whose social status had made them the arbiters of desirability. Tom, in other words, is not simply a rival who arrives inconveniently on the scene at some later point to contest a prize that Gatsby had already chosen on his own; he is, rather, the model of a desire that Gatsby has merely borrowed. For this reason, the story of his infatuation with Daisy is as "plagiaristic" as the revelations of the young men by whom Nick was besieged during his student days.

Nick, however, resists recognizing the borrowed quality of Gatsby's desire, and tries to locate the emotional backbone of his story in Gatsby's so-called "heightened sensitivity to the promises of life" (6). At the end of his narrative, Nick evokes the image of the Dutch sailors as they arrived in the New World. However, in a move whose curiousness has completely escaped critical attention, he identifies this *group* of sailors with the *solitary figure* of Gatsby at the moment "when he first picked out the green light at the end of Daisy's dock" (189). A more logical, as well as more revelatory, association, would have been between these Dutch sailors and the "excited young officers from Camp Taylor" (79) who were also pursuing Daisy during that summer in Louisville. Having missed this opportunity to high-light the mimetic implications of the celebrated image with which his narrative concludes, Nick credulously invites his readers to con-template a pristine, non-rivalistic world in which an unproblematic object "commensurate to the [human] capacity for wonder" (189), such as Gatsby thought that he had found in Daisy, did once exist. He thus fails to point our attention to the inextricable connection between Gatsby's own "capacity for wonder" and the male rivalry that necessarily accompanies it. The fact that Gatsby's fate is essentially that of a man whose *model*, in the form of Tom Buchanan, has also become his *rival* implies that Nick Carraway, far from clarifying, has actually obscured the central moral truth of his story. Furthermore, the Nick Carraway that Fitzgerald shows us at the end of the novel, far from being a reliable observer, is as morally obtuse and ethically blameworthy as any of the characters whom he subjects to his self-serving judgments.[3]

The traditional assumption—that the essential significance of *Gatsby* rests either with the magnificence of Gatsby's dream or the lu-cidity of Nick's understanding that it must be renounced—ignores the fact that both the emotional impact of the novel and its moral complexity arise primarily from the sacrificial ritual that it stages. Gatsby, whom Nick idealizes as a romantic hero, is, more pertinently to the pattern of events in the novel, also a scapegoat. Not only does he, in the most obvious sacrificial way, die in place of Daisy Bu-chanan. As importantly, he is, throughout the novel, the surrogate through whom Nick will experience romantic adventures vicariously while avoiding their potentially lethal consequences.[4]

Intimations of this pattern, which creates the covert scapegoating ritual that forms the otherwise missing emotional backbone of the novel as a whole, may be noted as early as its opening pages, in which Nick makes several allusions to his own insecurities. His first sen-tence refers to his "younger and more vulnerable years." He then al-ludes to his having been made the "victim of not a few veteran bores" and having been "unjustly accused of being a politician" (5). The role of victim, however, is almost immediately transferred to Gatsby, whom Nick describes on the following page as "preyed on," and ulti-mately destroyed, by the "foul dust [that] floated in the wake of his dreams" (6). Gatsby's romantic dream of reliving the past with Daisy will fail. However, Nick Carraway's dream—of maintaining his position of moral superiority by transferring to others the responsibility for desires and actions that would compromise the inviolability of his self-image—succeeds magnificently. In this respect, Nick proves himself to be a worthy descendant of the founder of his family, a great uncle who, as he ingenuously informs us, "sent a substitute to the Civil War" (7).

The novel itself is replete with details that suggest that Nick, far from being the detached moral observer that he would like us to see in him, is as driven (albeit furtively) by his passions as is Gatsby. This is clearly implied by the famous passage where Nick, responding to Gatsby's description of walking with Daisy on a summer's evening in Louisville, finds within himself a mirroring emotion: "Through all he said, even through his appalling sentimentality I was reminded of something—an elusive rhythm, a fragment of lost words, that I had heard somewhere a long time ago" (118).

Nick does not elaborate on this incomplete epiphany because the words that are about to be spoken disappear and "what I had almost remembered was uncommunicable forever." He does, however, provide a strikingly revelatory image of himself in a much less noticed passage in the novel that points unmistakably to his desire to conceal illicit passions:

> I began to like New York, the racy, adventurous feel of it at night and the satisfaction that the constant flicker of men and women and machines gives to the restless eye. I liked to walk up Fifth Avenue and pick out romantic women from the crowd and imagine that in a few minutes I was going to enter into their lives, and *no one would ever know or disapprove.* Sometimes, in my mind, I followed them to their apartments on the corners of hidden streets, and they turned and smiled back at me before they faded through a door into warm darkness. (61; emphasis added).

This passage—while commented on much less frequently than those that evoke Gatsby's dream or demonstrate Nick's presumed moral awareness—expresses with unmistakable conviction the emotional backbone that Fitzgerald thought he had failed to provide for *Gatsby.* With Gatsby as his go-between Nick will indeed enter the life of a "ro-

mantic" woman in a way that, while arguably meriting moral censure, will, with few exceptions, incite only respect and admiration on
the part of the novel's countless readers.

The myriad absurdities in the novel's plot to which its more perceptive critics, such as H. L. Mencken and L. P. Hartley, have objected (but which are resolved once we recognize that the purpose
of the plot is to advance Nick's dream) begin with Gatsby's arriving
on the scene with the resolve to do precisely what Nick fears to do
because it is morally compromising. Rather than risk harm to himself he blithely sends Gatsby off on a romantic adventure. The description that he then gives us of Gatsby's liaison with Daisy, while
lacking much by way of actual details, will convince us unmistakably
of the vicarious pleasure that it affords him. Toward the end of the
novel, not only Gatsby, but also Tom and Daisy, will be enlisted as
Nick's surrogates. Gatsby will be punished for the romantic dream
that he had pursued in Nick's stead. Thus, Nick will impute to him,
in the moments immediately preceding his death, the ultimate spiritual agony of contemplating the destruction of his romantic dream:
"He must have looked up at an unfamiliar sky through frightening
leaves and shivered as he found what a grotesque thing a rose is and
how raw the sunlight was upon the scarcely created grass" (169).
Gatsby "must" think such thoughts before he dies (even if the rhetorical flourish that conveys them cannot be attributed to him with
any plausibility) because, fundamentally, his role is to take upon
himself a shattering experience that would otherwise have been
Nick's. Nick will subsequently deflect attention from his own role
in Gatsby's death by insisting that Tom and Daisy were uniquely
responsible: "They were careless people, Tom and Daisy—they
smashed up things and creatures and then retreated back into their
money or their vast carelessness or whatever it was that kept them
together, and let other people clean up the mess they had made . . .
" (188). This pillorying of Tom and Daisy—who are not, to be sure,
blameless—artfully absolves Nick of any responsibility for Gatsby's
downfall.

Nick's mythologizing explanations aside, Gatsby's dream fails in
actual fact because two of its principal figures choose not to play the
roles that he has assigned to them: Daisy will not leave her husband
for Gatsby, nor will Tom passively acquiesce in the plans that Gatsby
has made for her. Gatsby, however, does play the roles that Nick has

chosen for him by acting upon the guilty desires that Nick could acknowledge only at the cost of losing his moral advantage; he then takes upon himself the punishment that Nick would have suffered had these desires been discovered. Furthermore, at the time of Gatsby's death, Tom and Daisy will behave in a sufficiently repellent fashion to sustain the burden of moral guilt that Nick wants to transfer to them. Finally, nearly all of the guests who took advantage of Gatsby's hospitality during the summer betray him by failing to attend his funeral, thus leaving Nick—who confides to us that he "began to have a feeling of defiance, of scornful solidarity between Gatsby and me against them all" (173)—with the deeply flattering image of himself as Gatsby's lone faithful standard-bearer.

Fitzgerald has, in other words, while bringing Gatsby's dream to a tragic conclusion, given Nick Carraway precisely the outcome that serves his own unacknowledged desires. Of course, since Nick's dream is fulfilled, he never has to face the shattering moment of moral insight that he projects upon Gatsby, whereby the latter, just before George Wilson murders him, finally realizes that "he had lost the old warm world, paid a high price for living too long with a single dream" (169). Nick will portentously conclude that his story amounts to a monitory lesson that the "orgastic future" of wish-fulfillment is irrevocably lost in the past. However, with an irony that entirely escapes him, it actually proves the contrary.

Nick's dream of concealing morally compromising behavior can, indeed, be achieved on condition that other people be made to pay the price. Gatsby, Tom, and Daisy must bear the burden of the guilty desires that Nick can only fleetingly acknowledge because they would require a painful reassessment of his moral nature. Thanks to their cooperative behavior, Nick's dream—of confirming through his own example the validity of his father's observation that "a sense of the fundamental decencies is parcelled out unequally at birth" (6)—remains intact. He subsequently invites readers of his tendentious narrative to contribute to the sustaining of his own self-aggrandizing legend. Thus, the Nick Carraway whom we see at the end of the novel is little different from the callow undergraduate who, by his own admission, devoted himself to the writing of "a series of very solemn and obvious editorials for the 'Yale News'" (8).

It is worth remembering that, in Fitzgerald's original conception of the novel Daisy's romantic lover was to be Nick Carraway. In creating the figure of Gatsby, he effectively distanced Nick from the experiences that he had originally intended for him, a point that is usually interpreted in terms of the moral detachment with which it provides Nick Carraway. A more important consequence, however, is that this distance allows Nick to pretend that the motivations at work within his story are not his own, but rather those of other people, who will then become the objects of his moral critique. So committed is he to this view of his story, and so appealingly does he present it to his readers, that it is extremely difficult for them to recognize that these characters are actually surrogates upon whom Nick projects an otherwise unsettling and, thus, morally unacceptable, image of himself. The final version of *Gatsby* is as much about Nick's dream as was the original. The nature of the dream, however, has shifted: the original fantasy of romantic possession has been assigned to Gatsby, where it will achieve poignant yet, finally, secondary, significance. Nick's dream, originally of a romantic nature, will now become the desire to experience guilty pleasures vicariously and to protect himself from pain, whether caused by his being rebuffed by a desirable woman, defeated in the struggle with a male rival, or subjected to moral censure by his society at large.

The absurdities that potentially mar the plot of the final version of *Gatsby* are not, for this reason, arbitrary or unintentional. They occur at moments where Fitzgerald offers us a glimpse of his original conception of the novel and thus of the motivations that involve Nick so intimately in the life of the man whose role is essentially to spare him the various indignities to which he would have been subjected had he acted on his own desires. After experiencing first the ecstasy and then the agony of acting on forbidden desires through Gatsby, Nick takes the further step of dealing retributive punishment to Tom and Daisy, denouncing them for their role in Gatsby's death with a vehemence and rhetorical effectiveness that have prevented generations of readers from raising questions about his own complicity and about the obsession with his own moral purity that motivates his condemnation of characters who are no more guilty than himself.

The habit of assuming that Gatsby's desire to "turn the clock back" with Daisy is the central motor of the novel—to which the behavior of other characters is merely reactive—will make it difficult for most readers readily to assent to the idea that this fantasy serves in the novel largely as a vehicle through which Nick's covert desires gain the expression that they cannot hope to achieve through direct means. Nevertheless, one detail of the plot—upon which all subsequent events of the novel depend—clearly reveals the existence of an unacknowledged desire that decisively influences Nick's behavior. This occurs in the scene in which Jordan Baker proposes to Nick the possibility of serving as Gatsby and Daisy's go-between.

Nick had earlier described himself as "full of interior rules that act as brakes on my desires" (63–64). However, after the long prelude in which Jordan fills Nick in on the background to Daisy's relationships with Gatsby and Tom before asking him to arrange the reunion, he replies "Did I have to know all this before he could ask such a little thing?" (84). The oddity of Nick's referring to his role in pandering to his neighbor's desire for an adulterous relationship with his cousin as "such a little thing" has largely eluded Fitzgerald's critics. Curiously, it is Gatsby himself who expresses some reservations at this idea. As Jordan tells Nick, Gatsby worried that Nick might be offended by the proposal. He even thought "to abandon the whole idea" (84) when he discovered that Nick and Tom are close friends, as though he expected this relationship to add a further impediment.

Fitzgerald underlines Nick's complete readiness to play the role of go-between when, in his subsequent conversation with Gatsby, he becomes clearly more insistent than Gatsby himself about arranging the reunion:

> "I talked with Miss Baker," I said after a moment. "I'm going to call Daisy tomorrow and invite her over here to tea."
> "Oh, that's all right," he said carelessly. "I don't want to put you to any trouble"
> "What day would suit you?"
> "What day would suit *you*?" he corrected me quickly. "I don't want to put you to any trouble, you see."
> "How about the day after tomorrow?" (87)

Fitzgerald implies that Nick has not entirely lost his moral bearings when, a moment later, Gatsby makes him a business proposal. Without even inquiring as to the details, Nick reacts in a way that suggests his moral alarm: "because the offer was obviously and tactlessly for a service to be rendered, I had no choice except to cut him off there" (88). Curiously, the compunction that Nick feels about accepting a vague, and not necessarily illicit, business proposal does not apply to his accepting a mission which is, beyond any doubt, morally compromising. Far from quailing at the dubious role that has been proposed to him, Nick tells us, in fact, that "[t]he evening had made me light-headed and happy" (88). He has, to be sure, just consented to a course of action that will, throughout the remainder of the novel, fulfill his double-dream of concealment and invulnerability to perfection.

Nick's description of the actual reunion—which takes place, as planned, at his home—encourages speculation that he has arranged it at least as much for his own benefit as for Gatsby's. We notice, for example, that he invites Daisy on the pretext of her having tea with him, a subterfuge that has no realistic motivation. He is subsequently the one who insists that Gatsby, who is convinced that she won't appear, continue waiting for Daisy: "He sat down miserably, *as if I had pushed him*" (90; emphasis added). Even the detail of the reunion's taking place in Nick's house suggests the presence of a subliminal desire. We are expected to believe, not only that Gatsby absolutely needs Nick in order to be reunited with Daisy, but that the meeting must take place in Nick's house because Gatsby wants Daisy to first see his own house from a distance! Beneath these patent absurdities in the plot, we may detect the workings of a covert desire that stages Gatsby's reunion with Daisy in such a way as to bring Nick as close as possible to fulfilling his own desire to possess a "romantic woman."

As in their first meeting at the Buchanans', the flirtatious overture will be made by Daisy, who greets Nick by asking if she had to come without Tom because they are lovers: "'Are you in love with me?' she said low in my ear. 'Or why did I have to come alone'" (90). Although Nick does not respond to Daisy's flirtatiousness, he had, a moment earlier, paid implicit homage to her erotic appeal when describing her leaving her car: "The exhilarating ripple of her voice was a wild tonic in the rain. I had to follow the sound of it for a moment, up and down, with my ear alone before any words came through. A damp streak of hair lay like a dash of blue paint across her cheek and her hand was wet with glistening drops as I took it to help her from the car" (90). When Gatsby enters the living room where Daisy awaits him, Nick suddenly becomes "[a]ware of the loud beating of my own heart" (91). When Gatsby then threatens to spoil the reunion by following Nick into the kitchen to declare, "[t]his is a terrible mistake" (92), Nick is the one who insists that it continue as planned: "'You're acting like a little boy,' I broke out impatiently. 'Not only that but you're rude. Daisy's sitting in there all alone"' (93). Such details as these require that we see in Nick something more than a mere go-between; clearly, he is as much the instigator as he is the instrument of the reunion between Gatsby and Daisy. He had described Tom Buchanan (at the time of their first meeting at his home in East Egg) as compelling "me from the room as though he were moving a checker to another square" (16). However, when the emotional stakes are sufficiently high, Nick shows himself to be equally capable of exerting control over his vicarious surrogate.

Nick's other covert motivations involve Tom Buchanan, who invokes in him intense feelings of resentment which, like his passion for Daisy, conflict with the pristine image of his moral nature that he is intent upon preserving. He cannot resist divulging his envy of Tom, and the feelings of inferiority that he arouses, whenever the latter comes within range. At such moments, the aura of implausibility that frequently surrounds the behavior of the novel's main characters entirely disappears. Readers who experience difficulty in believing in a hardened gangster who goes to his death for the love of his "one time sweetheart," will have no such difficulty in accepting Nick's entirely convincing, if largely inadvertent, rendering of the envious feelings that Tom arouses in him. Nick persuasively alludes to the grudging awe that Tom inspires in him, for example, in his recollection of the latter's having "come east in a fashion that rather took your breath away . . . It was hard to realize that a man in my own generation was wealthy enough to do that" (10).

Nick will try to damn Tom with a cunningly crafted verbal put-down when he attempts to dismiss him with the remark that he was "one of those men who reach such an acute limited excellence at twenty-one that everything afterwards savours of anti-climax" (10). Such one-upmanship cannot, however, entirely defend Nick from constantly feeling defeated by Tom, whose physical presence— which seems to say "don't think my opinion on these matters is final . . . just because I'm stronger and more of a man than you are" (11)—has no need of mere words.

Thanks to Gatsby, Nick will exact at least vicarious and provisional revenge against Tom. Fitzgerald allows him to savor the expectation of victory over Tom in the scene at the Buchanans' home that he places just before the Plaza Hotel episode. After Tom has left the room, Daisy "got up and went over to Gatsby, and pulled his face down kissing his mouth. 'You know I love you,' she murmured'" (122–23). Nick responds with obvious relish to the signs of Tom's imminent defeat: "She had told him [Gatsby] that she loved him, and Tom Buchanan saw. He was astounded. His mouth opened a little and he looked at Gatsby and then back to Daisy as if he had just recognized her as someone he knew a long time ago" (125). The next step in the orchestration of Tom's defeat occurs when, on the way to Manhattan, he stops at George Wilson's garage, where he learns that George and Myrtle are leaving for the West. At this point, Nick, believing that the vicarious triumph for which he has worked is finally within reach, expresses his exultation in a metaphor that leaves its sadistic motivation beyond any doubt: "As we drove away Tom was feeling *the hot whips of panic*. His wife and his mistress, until an hour ago secure and inviolate, were slipping precipitately from his control"(131; emphasis added).

At the end of the novel—with his victory undermined by Daisy's "betrayal" of Gatsby in her decision to return to her husband and daughter—Nick resorts again to the technique of attempting to diminish Tom by attacking him with a dismissive phrase. Meeting his adversary on Fifth Avenue, where his resentment is once again provoked by the sight of Tom walking "in his alert aggressive way, his hands out a little from his body as if to fight off interference, his head moving sharply here and there" (186), Nick discovers his moral advantage in knowing something that Tom apparently doesn't, i.e., that Daisy was driving Gatsby's car when it ran over Myrtle Wilson. Nick savors his triumph by contemplating the enormous difference in maturity that he imagines to exist between Tom and himself: "I shook hands with him; it seemed silly not to, for I felt suddenly as though I were talking to a child" (188). In order to appreciate the compensatory role of the wish-fulfilling fantasy that is at work in this remark, we need only remember the many other moments in the novel where Nick spontaneously experiences feelings of *inferiority* in Tom's presence. Once again, we find Nick gaining, in the realm of after-the-fact commentary, an advantage that he characteristically avoids trying to achieve in an actual confrontation with his adversary. Because of Nick's self-protective reticence on this point, we can only speculate as to just how soundly he may have been defeated by Tom Buchanan had he not decided so peremptorily that "[t]here was nothing I could say, except the one unutterable fact that it wasn't true" (187).

This scene also affords Nick an unexpected triumph in the form of the discovery that he and Daisy are bound together in secret intimacy by their knowledge—from which Tom Buchanan, along with every other living character in the novel, has apparently been excluded—of the true circumstances of Myrtle Wilson's death. This is not quite the achievement that Nick had dreamed about while walking at night on Fifth Avenue, but it does combine the motifs of a "romantic woman" and a hidden, illicit action of which "no one would ever know or disapprove" in an approximate and reasonably satisfying manner. In this way it provides a compensatory riposte to Nick's aggrieved recognition that, in reality, it is Tom and Daisy who can claim "membership in a rather distinguished secret society" (22) and a postmortem victory on Gatsby's behalf against Tom Buchanan, who had taunted his rival at the Plaza Hotel with the stinging boast that "there're things between Daisy and me that you'll never know" (140). Of course, it never occurs to Nick that his using Gatsby as an instrument for the satisfaction of his own desires—to possess a "romantic" woman and to defeat a redoubtable male rival in such a way that his own actions would escape detection—may place him in the company of the "foul dust" that rose around Gatsby's dreams. Nor has any critic of the novel ever suggested so negative of view of Nick's role. Generations of readers have, on the contrary, almost unanimously ratified the distinction that Nick would like to maintain between such "careless" people as Tom and Daisy and such a fundamentally "honest" person as himself.

In his 1989 study of *The Great Gatsby,* Richard Lehan assembled a number of comments by critics that illustrate the virtually unchallenged success that Nick's displacement of blame has enjoyed since the novel's publication in 1925. Marius Bewley, for example, denounces Daisy for her "vicious emptiness." Robert Ornstein finds her "criminally amoral" and Alfred Kazin characterizes her as "vulgar and inhuman." Lehan himself castigates Tom Buchanan in his spirited denunciation of the sad fact that sacrificial victims must die in order that "the Buchanan way of life can go on." He then extends this condemnation to an entire social class in his affirmation that the rich "are the ultimate source of romantic depletion" (*Great Gatsby*, 79).

Giles Mitchell expands this list of moral pariahs to include Gatsby himself, in whom he detects the failings of a person who suffers from a narcissistic personality, a judgment that leads him to criticize Gatsby for a lack of moral discernment in his desire to marry the already-married Daisy: "There is no evidence in the novel that Gatsby feels any moral conflict about urging Daisy to marry him—to marry into a life supported by criminal activities. . . . It is of crucial importance to note that Gatsby evinces no conscious sense of guilt for deceiving Daisy. Furthermore, there is no hint in the novel that he feels guilt unconsciously" ("Great Narcissist," 390). Mitchell's criticism of Gatsby could, of course, be equally applied to Nick Carraway, who deceives Daisy into thinking that he has invited her to his house in order to have tea with him and who, rather than evincing any reluctance, aggressively pursues arrangements for the adulterous relationship between Gatsby and Daisy. At no point in his disquisition on Gatsby's morally devious behavior, however, does Mitchell consider Nick's resemblance to Gatsby in this respect.

Yet another implicit exoneration of Nick's behavior occurs in Ernest Lockridge's intriguing essay, "F. Scott Fitzgerald's *Trompe l'Oeil* and *The Great Gatsby's* Buried Plot." Lockridge's basic argument is that Nick "is not to be trusted in his judgments and interpretations" (163). He adduces any number of details from the novel that, in his view, Nick has misunderstood. These range from the relatively uncontroversial suggestion that Nick is often deceived about himself, through the perceptive judgment that Daisy uses Gatsby to incite Tom's jealousy and a renewal of his marital fidelity, to the highly speculative assertion that Gatsby was murdered, not by George Wilson, but by order of Meyer Wolfsheim, who has been put "at great risk" by "Gatsby's indiscretion in flagrantly fooling around with another man's wife" (176). At no point in this ingenious, and seemingly exhaustive, analysis of the novel's covert plots, however, does Lockridge subject Nick to anything more than misgivings as to his reliability. The judgments of all these critics tend to confirm Nick's success in imposing his dream of personal moral innocence on the materials of his story, quite unlike Gatsby whose materials—particularly in the form of Tom and Daisy—proved to be ultimately recalcitrant. By directing their own moral condemnation exclusively toward the characters whom Nick himself had chosen as his scapegoats, they obediently speak the lines that he has given them.

Judith Fetterley is one of the few critics who has been willing to censure Nick for something more than the uncertainty of his moral judgment. She accuses him, more seriously, of a tendentious readiness to apply a "double standard" that consistently works to the disfavor of the female characters of the novel, turning them effectively into the novel's preferred scapegoats. According to Fetterley, Nick's report on Daisy's account of her unhappy relationship with Tom assures that her "suffering is reduced to a pose, and her vision of what it means to be born female is defined as a gimmick to exact tribute. Daisy may cry over Gatsby's shirts, but Nick has seen to it that no tears will be shed over her" (*Resisting Reader,* 85). Similarly, Jordan Baker, portrayed as "careless and indifferent to the existence of anyone else," qualifies for inclusion "in the foul dust that floats in the wake of Gatsby's death" (89). Fetterley also observes Nick's tendency to make absolute distinctions in places where underlying similarities are equally in evidence: "Nick exemplifies the cultural double standard in that he judges the behavior of men and women quite differently. He blames Jordan for relatively minor dishonesties, yet he accepts Gatsby's massive dishonesties with understanding. Nick would never call Gatsby's detours around the fact of his past dishonesty, for in Nick's eyes Gatsby's behavior is floated clear upon the floodtide of Nick's empathy with its sources" (94).

Fetterley, however, restricts her criticism of Nick to the charge of male chauvinism. The Nick who is willing to make *any* character in the novel a complicitous actor in the plot that he has designed to confirm his moral superiority thus escapes her otherwise penetrating critique. Fetterley's focus on Nick's presumably exclusive choice of female victims of discredited male romantic fantasies leads to her highly questionable assertion that Gatsby is not treated as a scapegoat in the novel as well as to her largely negative final judgment of *The Great Gatsby* itself, whose "much touted universality" she rejects because this consists finally in its fictional representation of "[t]he structures of the romantic imagination . . . [which] are affairs of the male ego from which women are excluded" (99). Although Fetterley's critique does have the great virtue of recognizing that the emotional backbone of the novel is to be found in the sacrificial ritual that it enacts, she seriously underestimates the importance of Gatsby's role as a surrogate victim. Gatsby does literally die in place of Daisy, who was responsible for the accident in which Myrtle Wilson was killed. He also dies in place of Tom Buchanan, who may have been killed if he had not directed George Wilson to Gatsby, as the car's real owner. In fact, as I suggested earlier, the mythic resonances of the novel as well as the overwhelming emotional effect that *The Great Gatsby* is still capable of provoking are largely due to the presence in the novel of a sacrificial motif.[5] If Gatsby had not died as a scapegoat, it is difficult to believe that we would still be reading Fitzgerald's novel eighty years after its publication.

Unlike Conrad and Ford who, in *Heart of Darkness* and *The Good Soldier*, encourage in the reader a certain ironic distance from their narrators, Fitzgerald seems, rather, to promote a close identification between Nick Carraway and his readers. Critics tend, for this reason, to take Nick's division of the world into saints and sinners at face value. The novel itself, however, is structured in such a way as to erode precisely those firm distinctions that he would maintain. Lionel Trilling once noted, in a related way, the curious weakening of gender boundaries in the novel when he characterized Jordan Baker as "vaguely homosexual" and McKee as "a pale feminine man" (quoted in Wasiolek, "Sexual Drama," 16). Patricia Thornton observes, in a related way, that the names of the guests who attended Gatsby's parties qualifies them as "sexual hybrids."[6] The women are masculinized (Mrs. Ulysses Swett, Frances Bull, etc.) while the men are feminized (Newton Orchid, Ernest Lilly, etc.). She further sees Nick as an essentially androgynous character by reason of his masculine pursuit of wealth and his feminine qualities of nurture and warmth.

The motif of "androgynous twins" (the term that Thornton applies to Nick and Jordan) infiltrates other, nonsexual relationships in the novel as well. Fitzgerald has, in fact, taken advantage of every possible opportunity to blur the distinction between characters whose radical dissimilarity would otherwise seem beyond challenge. The blurring of sexual distinctions is only a special instance of a broader phenomenon that can be observed even in details of the novel's setting. As Nick amusingly informs us, from the point of view of its "wingless" inhabitants, no two places could be more different than East and West Eggs, while the bird's-eye view hardly allows of any distinction between them:

> Twenty miles from the city a pair of enormous eggs, identical in contour and separated only by a courtesy bay, jut out into the most domesticated body of salt water in the Western Hemisphere, the great wet barnyard of Long Sound. They are not perfect ovals—like the egg in the Columbus story they are both crushed flat at the contact end—but their physical resemblance must be a source of perpetual confusion to the gulls that fly overhead. To the wingless a more arresting phenomenon is their dissimilarity in every particular except shape and size. (9)

In a parallel way, it is relatively easy to discern, beneath the superficial contrast between Gatsby and Tom, a deep affinity. Beyond the obvious fact that they are both competing for Daisy, they both also suffer from a sense of anticlimax in their lives. Gatsby wants to turn the clock back to a time when Daisy—with whom he imagined himself "gulping down the milk of wonder" (117)—appeared to be entirely his, and Tom, Nick tells us, "would drift on forever seeking a little wistfully for the dramatic turbulence of some irrecoverable football game" (10). Even the first glimpses that Nick has of Tom—"standing with his legs apart on the front porch" (11)—and of Gatsby—"standing with his hands in his pockets regarding the silver pepper of the stars" (25)—implies a submerged connection between the novel's two principal adversaries.

Likewise Gatsby and Myrtle, who appear to be such dissimilar characters, will implicitly mirror each other's social climbing. Gatsby's acquisition of the whole panoply of upper-class signifiers, including his signature affectation of addressing acquaintances as "old sport," will be unmistakably replayed, albeit in a minor key, in the transformation that overtakes Myrtle when she arrives in Manhattan with Tom:

> Mrs. Wilson had changed her costume some time before and was now attired in an elaborate afternoon dress of cream colored chiffon which gave out a continual rustle as she swept about the room. With the influence of the dress her personality had also undergone a change. The intense vitality that had

been so remarkable in the garage was converted into impressive hauteur. Her laughter, her gestures, her assertions became more violently affected moment by moment and as she expanded the room grew smaller around her until she seemed to be revolving on a noisy, creaking pivot through the smoky air. (35)

Fitzgerald's expansion of the category of "hybrid twins" to include the blurring of distinctions in social class also appears in one of the most curious descriptions of a character in the novel, which occurs when Myrtle, having just arrived in Manhattan with Tom, pleads with him to buy her a dog. Significantly, Fitzgerald imbues this brief, and entirely secondary, scene with elements that mirror the proliferation of hybrids that is observable throughout the novel. Myrtle wants a "police dog." The salesman, offering her a dog that Tom authoritatively identifies as "no police dog," admits that "it's not exactly a police dog." Nick creates some uncertainty regarding the salesman's subsequent claim that "[i]t's more of an Airedale" by observing, "undoubtedly there was an Airedale concerned in it somewhere though its feet were startlingly white" (32). The ensuing exchange concerning the sex of the dog—with the salesman assuring them that it is "a boy"—and Tom countering with at least equal conviction that "it's a bitch"—suggests that the androgyny that Thornton attributes to Nick and Jordan may have less to do with the sexual orientation of particular characters and more the structural tendency of the novel to undermine dichotomies of any sort. This dissolving of distinctions reaches its culmination in the description of the salesman himself: "a grey old man who bore an absurd resemblance to John D. Rockefeller" (31).

This recurrent discovery of similarities between people otherwise assumed to be radically unlike each other applies equally to the distinction that Nick would like to maintain between such a "careless" person as Daisy and such a fundamentally "honest" person as himself. He joins Daisy and Tom in contributing at the inquest to the cover-up of the real circumstances of Myrtle Wilson's death and guarantees that Gatsby's death will indeed bring a return to peacetime "normalcy" by refusing to enlighten Tom Buchanan on this same subject. As we have already noted, his return to the Middle West exactly mimics Tom and Daisy's retreat from the catastrophe for which all three are responsible. Amazingly, however, neither

Nick nor the vast majority of his readers recognize in him the mirror image of the couple upon whom he has chosen to displace the entire guilt. Our readiness to confirm Nick's claim to his having played an entirely innocent role in the events that he recounts is well exemplified by Elizabeth Morgan's enumeration of the successive betrayals to which Gatsby has been subjected in the course of the novel:

> Gatsby is cruelly duped. He is duped by Dan Cody (or at least his mistress) whose elegant lifestyle and "almost" legacy to his adopted vassal gave Gatsby a taste for easy money. He is duped by Daisy, who appears to love from above, but who, in fact, is incapable of love. He is duped by seeming courtiers and their mistresses who came to his palace for entertainment, but who later vacate his life as effortlessly as they came. He is duped by a sentimentalized rhetoric of love which his upbringing and brief, militarily sponsored stay at Oxford did not have the power to call into question. ("Gatsby in the Garden," 170)

Nowhere in this litany of denunciations, however, do we find the slightest hint that Gatsby's tragedy may in some way be linked to Nick's pandering, which miraculously escapes the censure that falls so copiously on other characters.

The reason for this discrepancy is surely to be sought in our unreflective susceptibility to accept the myth of moral innocence, which is much more deeply rooted and, for this reason, much more difficult to eradicate than Gatsby's merely romantic dream. The moral significance of the novel rests, not with the adolescent discovery that romantic dreams are no longer viable, but with our capacity to recognize the extent to which we have so readily allowed ourselves to be lured by Nick Carraway's construction of a fictional world that does respond perfectly to his own indestructible need to see himself as a thoroughly moral individual. Richard Anderson inadvertently alludes to this dimension of the novel when he observes:

> Like Gatsby, even the most hardheaded Americans conceive of themselves (whether correctly is not the point) as idealists whose dreams can be made true, as eternal youths whose innocence can never really be lost, as magicians who can mesmerize the world into accepting their dreams. Fitzgerald, in tapping that cultural myth, made *The Great Gatsby* an Ameri-

can—indeed, a world—classic, a persistent and permanent presence in American culture." (in Bruccoli, *New Essays*, 37)

Anderson is right in suggesting that the power of the novel derives from its tapping into a profound myth, but wrong in identifying Gatsby as the principal vehicle of this myth. It is, after all, Nick who transforms the characters of his story into aspects of his own personality that conflict with the good opinion of himself to which he is so strongly attached and then returns to the Middle West with his moral innocence intact. Contrary to Anderson, who maintains that it matters little whether or not we are right in holding to this dream of innocence, the novel points compellingly, in fact, to the unacceptable moral and human costs that it entails.

Fitzgerald's rendering of scapegoating in *The Great Gatsby* is not, to be sure, limited to the behavior of his narrator. Rather, he places Nick's characteristic activity of transferring blame to others against the background of a human community that mirrors this procedure. Nick resorts to scapegoating in order to protect the self-esteem that he needs in order to fashion for himself a livable life; his community finds in it, despite its moral dubiousness, a socially useful ritual violence through which it protects itself against much more damaging forms of violence. While Nick's efforts to convince us that Gatsby's personal attributes justify his calling him "great" are never wholly satisfactory, Gatsby does in fact achieve a kind of greatness, albeit unwittingly, through his structural role as the innocent victim who preserves the stability of his community through his sacrificial death. The creative inspiration that, by his own admission, deserted Fitzgerald when he attempted to render the reunion between Gatsby and Daisy emerges with great force when he turns to scenes involving the relationship between a community and a designated individual who has become the privileged object of its attention. Nick alludes to this pattern from the beginning, when he describes himself as having been "unjustly accused of being a politician" during his student days and, even more suggestively, as "privy to the secret griefs of wild, unknown men" (5). The novel concludes, of course, with the famous evocation of the image of the group of Dutch sailors who are united by their contemplation of the "fresh, green breast of the new world" (189).

Fitzgerald will similarly resort to this pattern each time that he introduces one of his main characters. Thus, he describes Tom Buchanan, as having "been one of the most powerful ends that ever played football at New Haven" (10). Daisy, in her turn, is described as being "by far the most popular of all the young girls in Louisville" (79). Likewise, Nick will recognize Jordan Baker when meeting her for the first time because her "pleasing contemptuous expression had looked out at me from many rotogravure pictures of the sporting life at Asheville and Hot Springs and Palm Beach" (23). Even Gatsby—whose sights are supposed to be fixed exclusively on Daisy —reveals his even greater desrie to be seen in the public eye when he claims that, during the war, "I was promoted to be a major and every Allied government gave me a decoration—even Montenegro, little Montenegro down on the Adriatic Sea" (70). The human longing to attract the admiring attention of a large, anonymous group is evinced on an appropriately more modest scale by Nick Carraway himself, who had hoped while at Yale to achieve fame as a writer thanks to the "very solemn and obvious editorials" that he wrote for the student newspaper.

The fascination with figures who have attracted public attention also takes precedence over the novel's presumed focus on romantic love when Nick describes an ideal woman who seems, rather oddly, to be drawn, not from romantic novels, but from the world of billboard advertising: "Unlike Gatsby and Tom Buchanan I had no girl whose disembodied face floated along the dark cornices and blinding signs . . ." (85). Nick will allude to the tragic side of this same motif in rendering his final judgment of Gatsby, whom he characterizes as the isolated, innocent victim of a group of adversaries described as the "foul dust [that] floated in the wake of his dreams" (6).

Even Gatsby's romantic attachment to Daisy was precipitated by his discovery that she was, in the eyes of all the young men in Louisville, the most desirable prize. Jordan Baker will imply the precedence of the group's valuation of Daisy when she tells Nick that "excited young officers from Camp Taylor demanded the privilege of monopolizing her that night" (79). Gatsby will later confirm the importance of the group in establishing Daisy's value when he tells Nick that "[I]t excited him too that many men had already loved Daisy—it increased her value in his eyes" (156).

So attached is Fitzgerald to this image of an individual whose elevation in the eyes of the group by no means excludes his becoming the object of its aggression, that he will constantly resort to epithets linking Gatsby—"a son of God. . . [who] must be about his father's business" (104)—with the figure of Christ, however improbable this association may appear at first glance. As Douglas Taylor has intriguingly suggested, Fitzgerald repeatedly characterizes Gatsby and arranges the episodes leading ultimately to his death in order to imply quite precise parallels with the Gospel account of the passion and death of Christ. He further notices that the description of Gatsby's death itself is presented in such a way as to convey unmistakable undertones of a sacrificial ritual:

> Aside from the literal aspects of Gatsby's preparation for swimming and the manner of his death, the details which invest these final actions have a suggestiveness of tone that accommodates itself tenably to his ritualistic concept of piety and consecration: his bathing trunks, the finality and passivity of his movements, the appropriately autumnal season, his death on water and the slow, symbolic commingling of his blood with the pool's motion to describe within a revolving cluster of dead leaves "a thin red circle" on its surface carry strong overtones of a primitive kind of sacrificial readiness for death which, combined with the immediate factor of natural infertility and decline, echo something of the old animistic response to affliction and unrest, the ceremonious mutilation of life for spiritual salvation and renewal through the reintegrative mystery of death and transfiguration. (in Claridge, *F. Scott Fitzgerald*, 216)

Arguing that Fitzgerald uses these sacrificial allusions somewhat in the manner of Yeats and Eliot and Joyce "to alchemize the anarchy of modern life into a unity and permanence" (216) Taylor concludes that the effort itself must necessarily fail because modern Americans lack the "moral habits" of their ancestors, which gave efficacy to their ancient religious rituals. *Gatsby* may, however, be more plausibly interpreted as supporting the contrary conclusion. The Americans of Fitzgerald's novel—including Tom and Daisy, but also Nick—can be shown, in others words, to be every bit as hypocritical and self-deceived as the ancestors who resorted to the morally dubious practice of scapegoating.

Fitzgerald alludes to this sacrificial pattern even when it doesn't quite correspond to the facts of a given situation, as when he blames Gatsby's fall on "the foul dust," which suggests a much larger group of adversaries than could be reasonably accounted for. Even the "whole rotten bunch" may strike some readers as an excessively broad term to apply to the actually quite small number of characters in the novel who have behaved badly toward Gatsby. The most fascinating of these examples, however, occurs when Nick Carraway describes Gatsby's murder, which, although it is the work of one man, George Wilson, he characterizes as a public sacrificial ritual: "It was after we started with Gatsby toward the house that the gardener saw Wilson's body a little way off in the grass, and the holocaust was complete" (170).

Most readers would probably grant that Nick's surprising use of the word "holocaust" (which Fitzgerald misspells as "holycaust" in the manuscript) seriously distorts the actual circumstances of Gatsby's murder and Wilson's suicide. The double death is a purely private affair involving Gatsby and Wilson; it is also an *accidental* event, which would never have occurred if Wilson had known the true identity of his wife's killer. The word "holocaust" has a number of associations that seem entirely inappropriate to the scene that Nick has just observed. A holocaust is, to begin with, a planned, highly organized public event involving the sacrifice of some propitiatory object. As Fitzgerald's misspelling reminds us, holocausts have sacred, religious overtones: an offering is made to a divinity who, it is hoped, will reciprocate with some desirable blessing.

Figurative allusions to the communal acts of violence that are implied by the word "holocaust appear repeatedly throughout the novel: in Meyer Wolfsheim's cufflinks, for example, which are made of human molars (77), and in Nick's complaint about his being besieged by "wild, unknown men"—presumably, his casual acquaintances at Yale University, for whom the epithets "wild" and "unknown" may not have been entirely appropriate, except that they do serve Fitzgerald's purpose of evoking a milieu in which "holocausts" would have been a likely outcome. Yet another moment where verisimilitude recedes in order to accommodate this underlying pattern occurs when Nick explains the rationale for Gatsby's lavish parties. Fitzgerald creates a somewhat feeble, realistic motivation according to which these parties are an elaborate device concocted by Gatsby in the hope that Daisy might one night appear at one of them. Generations of readers have interpreted this detail as enhancing the aura of Gatsby's extravagant romanticism. It may, however, be more legitimately interpreted as showing the intensity of Fitzgerald's attachment to the pattern formed by the community and its isolated member.

Daisy never does accidentally wander into one of Gatsby's parties; hence, the parties themselves never once become the setting for their romantic reunion. They do, however, become the occasion for one of the most vivid renderings of the "all against one" motif in the novel, which occurs when Nick describes his seeing Gatsby standing in splendid isolation above the group of guests that his invitation has assembled:

> The nature of Mr. Tostoff's composition eluded me, because just as it began my eyes fell on Gatsby, standing alone on the marble steps and looking from one group to another with approving eyes. His tanned skin was drawn attractively tight on his face and his short hair looked as though it were trimmed every day. I could see nothing sinister about him. I wondered if the fact that he was not drinking helped to set him off from his guests, for it seemed to me that he grew more correct as the fraternal hilarity increased. (54)

Fitzgerald's intuitive grasp of the unity and coherence with which an isolated individual can invest a human community is further deepened by his characteristic tendency to juxtapose this pattern with one in which this same community is shown as divided into rivalistic factions. The most important rivalry is, to be sure, the one involving Gatsby and Tom Buchanan, who struggle for possession of Daisy. Fitzgerald has, guided by a profound intuition, set the story of their competition against the background of violence between groups, the most important historical example of which is the "Great War," which is associated a number of times with key events in the lives of the main characters. It provides the occasion that allows such midwesterners as Nick to escape their provincial origins. It also brings Gatsby within range of Daisy in Louisville and takes him from her when he receives orders sending him to Europe and, eventually, to Oxford. In a deeper way, however, World War I serves to remind the reader that male rivalry does not only lead to struggles for possession of a desirable woman. It can, on the contrary, if not adequately contained by an effective ritual, lead to a worldwide conflagration.

Fitzgerald evokes this possibility by having Nick allude metaphorically to combat between rival armies in the course of describing one of Gatsby's parties. Shortly after the scene in which the party-goers were formed into an organized, harmonious group by his "approving eyes," Gatsby disappears into his mansion. Nick now sees that in the absence of Gatsby, who has until then been the center of the group's attention (both as their host and as the object of titillating rumors), the party descends into chaos. Fitzgerald appropriately has Nick resort to a military metaphor that reminds us of the recently ended war, which is now being reenacted in miniature:

> I looked around. Most of the remaining women were now having fights with men said to be their husbands. Even Jordan's party, the quarter from East Egg, were *rent asunder by dissension.* One of the men was talking with curious intensity to a young actress, and his wife after attempting to laugh at the situation in a dignified and indifferent way broke down entirely and resorted to *flank attacks*—at intervals she appeared suddenly at his side like an angry diamond and hissed "You promised" into his ear. (56; emphasis added)

Yet another allusion to warfare—in this case, to a war specifically provoked by sexual rivalry—occurs at the beginning of chapter 5 where Nick launches into a three-page listing—amounting to a Homeric catalog—of the various guests who attended Gatsby's parties during the summer of 1922. The mock-heroic tone of this listing is unmistakable from the beginning:

> From East Egg, then, came the Chester Beckers and the Leeches and a man named Bunsen whom I knew at Yale and Doctor Webster Civet who was drowned last summer up in Maine. And the Hornbeams and the Willie Voltaires and a whole clan named Blackbuck who always gathered in a corner and flipped up their noses like goats at whosoever came near. And the Ismays and the Chrysties (or rather Hubert Auerbach and Mr. Chrystie's wife) and Edgar Beaver whose hair they say turned cotton-white one winter afternoon for no good reason at all. (66)

As the catalog continues, the ironic allusions to the anti-heroes of this gallery of characters recall the heroic cadences borrowed from epic accounts of violence, such as *The Iliad*, in which Helen of Troy—whose face, as Christopher Marlowe was later to write, "launched a thousand ships"—is the avatar of Daisy Buchanan.

Tom Buchanan adds a comic dimension to this motif in his concern about the threat posed by "coloured empires." Commenting on the title of the book, *The Rise of the Coloured Empires*, that has provoked this anxiety in Tom, Matthew J. Bruccoli explains, in his notes to the 1995 Scribner's edition of *Gatsby*, that while Fitzgerald's source was Lothrop Stoddard's *The Rising Tide of Color*, "it seems clear that Fitzgerald did not want to provide the correct title and author" (208). While informative, this remark does not do entire justice to Fitzgerald's stroke of genius in inventing for Tom's book the uncannily oxymoronic phrase "coloured empires." The uncanniness and troubling menace in Tom's eyes of a world that really did have "coloured empires" is a paranoid distortion of a legitimate fear of a world in which equally powerful rival factions competed for the same prize. The destructive violence of such a world is, as allusions to the recently concluded "Great War" remind us, not merely a paranoid's fantasy or a novelist's invention. While we no doubt find Tom Buchanan's racism repugnant, the "verbal hybrid" introduced by the title of his favorite book evokes a disquiet that goes much deeper than merely contemptible racial attitudes. It portends a world in which groups that once occupied distinct positions within a stable hierarchy that kept them from becoming rivals are now involved in the competitive struggle for possession of the same desirable object.

If, as René Girard maintains, the purpose of a ritual involving sacrificial expulsion is to prevent the spread of other, more destructive forms of violence that would threaten the well-being of the community as a whole, then "holocaust" becomes an unerringly precise description, not of George Wilson's personal motivations, but of the subliminal communal function served by Gatsby's murder. While the death of Gatsby is, on the level of the novel's surface plot, the result of an unfortunate and contingent mistake, it is a predetermined necessity for the underlying sacrificial pattern that the plot enacts. Gatsby must be selected as the sacrificial victim because—in spite of his great wealth and mobster connections—he is essentially an outsider, a man from an entirely other world, who lacks the support of associates willing to exact revenge against anyone (Tom Buchanan, for example) who may in some way be held responsible for his death.

Any other scenario that one could imagine following Myrtle's death would have led to a series of acts and counter-acts of violence. Nick's merely apparent malapropism thus points unerringly to the communal significance of Gatsby's death: a ritual act that restores the peace and well-being of a community that is not overly intent on examining too closely the legitimacy of the act that has brought it such benefits. This "holocaust" will, in turn, transform Gatsby, the "shady adventurer" of L. P. Hartley's dismissive judgment, into the tragic figure upon whose ultimate "greatness" Nick Carraway rightly, if somewhat obtusely, insists. As Nick will never recognize, but as the scapegoating pattern of the novel makes clear, the sobriquet that he so admiringly bestows on Gatsby is validated, not by the latter's personal attributes, but by the sacrificial role that he has been made to play.

Our recognition that Gatsby is objectively and undeniably "great" by reason of his role as an innocent sacrificial victim provides a much more secure justification for the novel's title than do the unpersuasive explanations advanced by Nick Carraway, or by the many critics who have followed in his wake, to account for Gatsby's *personal* greatness. I am thinking in particular of interpretations of the novel that require our accepting Gatsby's dream as anything more than a form of glorified plagiarism. Richard Anderson, for example, believes that Gatsby's ambition is based on a distinction, wholly unfounded in my view, between "crass material riches" and "fulfillment measured by realizing a dream; a romantic purity undefiled by Jay Gatsby's limitations when that dream turns to dust" (in Bruccoli, *New Essays*, 29). Robert Ornstein similarly asserts that "Gatsby *is* great because his dream, however naive, gaudy, and unattainable, is one of the grand illusions of the race, which keep men from becoming too old or too wise or too cynical of their human limitations" (in Claridge, *F. Scott Fitzgerald*, 245). Likewise, Brian Way maintains that the plagiaristic quality of Gatsby's dream in no way disqualifies it from our admiration: "By the close of the novel, Fitzgerald has completed his immensely difficult task of convincing us that Gatsby's capacity for illusion is poignant and heroic, in spite of the banality of his aspirations and the worthlessness of the objects of his dreams" (*Art of Social*

*Fiction,* 109–10). One may legitimately wonder, however, whether it is not the credulousness of the novel's readers—impelled by their strongly felt obligation to confirm Nick's positive evaluation of Gatsby's personal qualities—that creates the effect of poignancy that Way describes.

Gatsby's role in unifying the group—in giving shape to a human community that might otherwise descend into potentially boundless rivalistic violence—is confirmed in a curious way by the circumstances of his funeral, which Fitzgerald stages as an event more closely resembling a "holocaust" than did the actual circumstances of his death. For most readers, this is surely one of the most poignant moments in *The Great Gatsby.* The multitude of guests who had taken such advantage of his hospitality—making his parties the focal point of their romantic summer—entirely abandon him in the aftermath of his pathetic death. The poignancy of this painful turn of events should not, however, obscure the continuity that it signifies in terms of Gatsby's role as outsider. Whether Gatsby is embraced by the group or rejected by it is finally a matter of indifference. Quite apart from his romantic dreams, Gatsby has been chosen to play in the novel that bears his name a preeminently sacrificial role as the figure who will create unanimity among the members of the group that has both elevated and excluded him. For this reason, there is no essential difference between the living Gatsby who stands on the marble steps contemplating his assembled guests and the dead Gatsby from whom they all flee.

Fitzgerald underlines—in the course of staging the climactic moment of his novel as the reenactment of an ancient religious ritual—the hypocrisy that is fundamentally implicated in the form of behavior through which human communities achieve their equanimity and prosperity. Gatsby's death appears to be the result of a series of contingent events: his chivalrous decision to protect Daisy; Wilson's going to Tom for information about the car; and Tom's apparent ignorance as to who was driving Gatsby's car on the night of the accident that took Myrtle's life. In a deeper way, however, these successive acts are determined by an implicit rule that requires that an innocent outsider be substituted for the real yet untouchable culprit. Nick Carraway, who from one perspective is as guilty of scapegoating as any other character, does break ranks with his fellow spectators to Gatsby's "holocaust" in order to proclaim, at least to his readers, the news that Gatsby, perfectly innocent of any involvement in the death of Myrtle Wilson, died as a substitute victim. In this way, he performs a praiseworthy ethical service in preventing us as his readers from accepting with an easy conscience the basic dishonesty that this expeditious solution entails. At the same time, however, Nick has made his readers accomplices to another kind of sacrificial ritual whereby they impute entire responsibility for Gatsby's death to Tom and Daisy and, by casting them beyond the pale, create a catharsis that is as emotionally satisfying as it is morally questionable.

Gatsby could not turn the clock back because he constructed a dream whose success depended on the cooperation of other people: his misjudgment as to their motivations and likely behavior is tragically revealed in the episode at the Plaza Hotel, where both Tom and Daisy refuse to play the roles that he has assigned them. Unlike Gatsby, Nick successfully projects upon the other characters roles that they played to perfection: Gatsby gives him the vicarious satisfaction of possessing Daisy and of almost destroying Tom Buchanan; likewise, Tom and Daisy, while refusing ultimate victory to Gatsby, do offer it to Nick by bearing the burden, not only of their own moral responsibility, but of his as well. Finally, readers of the novel become accomplices to Nick's spurious achievement by admiring the preemptive moral elevation that he unfailingly attributes to himself.

In contrast to this dubious outcome, the genuinely moral dimension of *The Great Gatsby*—and, hence, its enduring greatness and universality—rests with the opportunity that it affords us to experience, yet also to resist, the scapegoating impulses that form—in a way that is, at once, both flagrant and surreptitious—its "emotional backbone." While it is difficult to believe that we continue to read *Gatsby* merely to learn what Nick thinks he has learned, the undiminished shock that we are capable of experiencing each time that we come to the pages devoted to the "holocaust" that has been prepared for Gatsby himself reveals the novel's perennial capacity for evoking in us feelings of moral unease about the performance of an atavistic social ritual in which we ourselves continue to be implicated.

# 5

## Ending Rituals in
### *To the Lighthouse*

THROUGHOUT *To THE LIGHTHOUSE*, VIRGINIA WOOLF REMINDS US OF the extent to which the unity and stability of a human community depend upon the willingness of its members to resort to sacrificial rituals. Toward the beginning of the novel, for example, she presents Mrs. Ramsay as thinking that "[i]f her husband *required sacrifices* (and indeed he did) she cheerfully *offered up to him* Charles Tansley, who had snubbed her little boy" (16; emphasis added). Tansley's function as a designated scapegoat is reaffirmed toward the end of the novel when Lily reflects on the pleasure that she experiences in "flagellating his lean flanks when she was out of temper" (197). In the course of the dinner party that provides the climactic moment of the first section of the novel, Woolf adds yet another element to this motif when she has Lily reflect on the pleasure that Mrs. Ramsay takes in leading "her victims . . . to the altar" (101). The dinner guests themselves will, after a very hesitant beginning, finally cohere as a group when the lighting of the candles unifies them in their "common cause" against the darkness outside. The bonding that occurs between Mr. Ramsay and James aboard the boat as it arrives at the lighthouse similarly involves the exclusion of James's sister Cam.

Val Gough, in "The Mystical Copula: Rewriting the Phallus in *To the Lighthouse*," has persuasively argued that the motif of a sacrificial act bringing some positive benefit to the community extends to the behavior of all of the principal characters in the novel. He observes, for example, that "Mrs. Ramsay's effort to bolster the male ego is represented in the novel as a process of virtual self-annihilation which, however, is simultaneously perceived by her to be an act of creation" (Hussey, *Virginia Woolf: Emerging Perspectives*, 218). More generally, he interprets the dinner party as "an event of female creativity which also involves a metaphoric sacrifice and consumption of the mother and other feminized and anti-phallic characters" (218). He finds additional sacrificial acts in William Bankes's decision to give up his solitude in order not to hurt Mrs. Ramsay and in Lily's avoidance of behavior that would provoke Charles Tansley's anger. To these examples must be added the fundamental exclusionary ritual—epitomized by Charles Tansley's whispered words to Lily Briscoe—"[w]omen can't paint, women can't write" (48)—that constitutes cultural activity as a traditionally male domain.[1]

At the same time that she implies the necessity of sacrificial practices, however, Woolf protests against their injustice, primarily through her portrayal of Lily Briscoe, who refuses to accept the particular form of exclusion that has been reserved for her as a woman. Lily's effort to transgress the boundary that separates her from an activity that has been historically coded as masculine is portrayed in a highly sympathetic manner in "The Window" by the narrator, who, at the end of the novel, shows Lily successfully completing a painting that is both an individual achievement and a sign of her having successfully violated the taboo that would have kept her from joining the company of her fellow painters.

However, Woolf's portrayal of Lily's triumph, and the blurring of gender distinctions that it involves, is recounted in a novel that, in other respects, registers her panicky reaction against precisely that dissolution of boundaries that she seems otherwise to approve. The "Time Passes" section, in particular, presents the disappearance of stable boundaries—between light and dark, earth and water, human and non-human, and, perhaps most significantly, male and female—as a catastrophe. The crossing of boundaries, which may, in its positive outcome, culminate in the "androgynous vision" that Woolf champions elsewhere, here produces a grotesquely hermaphroditic monster.[2]

Woolf implies that the chaos that she so vividly represents in this section of her novel (which includes the period of World War I) is produced when a society can no longer perform the acts of ritual expulsion upon which its stability depends. The order that had been created by the successful designation of these figures now collapses, thus giving way to a completely undifferentiated world in which, as Woolf's frequent resort to personification will imply, the distinction between the human and the non-human disappears. Similarly, the arrival at the Ramsay's home of perfect strangers—"trespassers," as the narrator calls them—portends the collapse of a reassuring boundary between those who belong to a particular group and those who do not. The crisis represented in this section is finally brought to an end thanks to the persistence of the one form of distinction— between members of different social classes—that survives the otherwise total dissolution represented in "Time Passes." Thus, like Mildred, the cook who prepares the Boeuf en Daube (the centerpiece of a dinner party that she will not herself attend), Mrs. McNab and Mrs. Bast restore order to the Ramsays' house in preparation for a homecoming in which they will take no further part.

"The Lighthouse" (the third and concluding section of the novel) resolves this tension—between Lily's transgressive aspirations and Woolf's conflicting recognition of the pragmatic necessity of maintaining barriers—by staging a double ending that simultaneously affirms and transcends the sacrificial ritual through which male privileges had been traditionally denied to women. This double ending reveals Woolf's effort to synthesize the opposing values of exclusion—the foundational act in the absence of which the community cannot exist—and inclusion, whereby the community seeks to integrate the outsiders whom it had initially excluded.[3] The first ending—in which Mr. Ramsay relinquishes the tiller to James— evokes the perennial cultural practice whereby the bond between father and son is affirmed by the exclusion of the sister. Cam may envy James his triumph, but she does not seriously challenge his claim to the tiller by presenting herself as his rival.

The second ending, with Lily completing her painting in the company of the poet Augustus Carmichael is, in effect, a rewriting of the historically sanctioned resolution that takes place in the boat. The otherwise unnecessary presence of Augustus Carmichael at this moment in the novel reveals Woolf's intent to mirror the scene of Cam's exclusion from the bond that unites father and son in order to underline the contrasting inclusion that Lily has achieved. It also allows her to draw a contrast between the pact that Cam had earlier formed with her brother James, from which Mr. Ramsay had been expelled, and the bond between Lily and Carmichael over which he, as the chief representative of productive cultural activity, must necessarily preside. Lily's individual achievement depends upon her learning to acknowledge the centrality of the inherited cultural tradition upon which her own activity as a painter depends. In order to attain this resolution, she must outgrow her own readiness to reject this tradition—embodied in its most exasperating form by Mr. Ramsay—and to affirm, however implicitly, her profound affinity with its male practitioners.

The sequence of endings implies that the father/son bond is indeed the privileged relationship through which the cultural inheritance is transmitted. Lily's triumph, however, demonstrates that the culturally constructed figure of the son is not, ultimately at least, reserved exclusively to the child who happens to be physically male. The completion of her painting inducts her into a form of fellowship with Augustus Carmichael from which the rivalry inherent in the relationship between Cam and James has disappeared. Lily and Carmichael become fellow artists who participate equally in the artistic role that has been bequeathed to them.[4] As Hermione Lee has observed, the figure who presides over this victory is Mr. Ramsay himself: "In a novel which criticizes and mocks but finally finds admirable Mr. Ramsay's bleak drama of endurance, the consolations offered for death are based on the real Mr. Ramsay's principles. Completed forms, whether made from a social and family group, an abstract painting, or the journey to the lighthouse, create the only lasting victory over death and chaos" (*Novels of Virginia Woolf,* 137).

Woolf's recognition of the contradiction inherent in a social practice that is both necessary and unjust aligns her novel with the others chosen for this study. She does, however, depart from the practice of her predecessors in one noticeable respect: whereas they had told their stories from the point of view of first-person narrators who also played important roles in the events that they recounted, Woolf creates an anonymous narrator who enters the minds of a variety of characters at will. In certain respects, this distinction does not seriously affect the underlying affinities that Woolf's novel shares with the others. The privileged access that this narrator enjoys to the private thoughts of her characters will, for example, produce a narrative whose subjective, psychological emphasis will remind us of the narratives of the first-person narrator/characters; at the same time, she will cast the thoughts of these characters in such a way as to hint at the sacrificial subtext of her novel. The voice adopted by Woolf's anonymous narrator, regardless of which characters' thoughts she has momentarily inhabited, is recognizably the same voice. The single narrative voice that we heard in *The Turn of the Screw, Heart of Darkness, The Good Soldier,* and *The Great Gatsby* has, in effect, been dispersed among a variety of characters without, however, losing its continuous preoccupation with scapegoating, which it ambiguously criticizes and practices.

Woolf's narrator is, however, different in one significant respect: unlike the governess, Marlow, Dowell, and Nick Carraway, she possesses an understanding of her story that cannot be improved upon by her readers. The stories told to us by each of these earlier narrators—particularly with respect to the proper interpretation of their sacrificial subtexts—contained fundamental mistakes or mystifications that had to be corrected by a reader, who was aided in this undertaking by implicit, demystifying signals left by the authors themselves. In Woolf's novel, however, the narrator's rejection of ritual exclusion is so thoroughgoing that she ultimately resists the temptation (which is nonetheless a palpable presence throughout her narrative) to construct *any* of her characters as a credible scapegoat. No single character in *To the Lighthouse* is constructed as an outsider in the eyes of the novel's readers in quite the same way as the substitute scapegoats that we encountered in previous chapters. On the contrary, the significantly more enlightened narrator of *To the Lighthouse* is careful to exculpate any character likely to arouse persecutory ire in the minds of her readers. Charles Tansley and Mr. Ramsay, in particular, become objects of her solicitude in a way that was simply unthinkable in the earlier novels. Thus, she will have not only Mrs. Ramsay but also her daughter Cam as well as Lily Briscoe think of these male characters in ways that liberate them from the sacrificial role for which they had otherwise been designated. As a result, the clues that, in our other novels, we must look for outside the narrative discourse are, in *To the Lighthouse,* contained within it.

As I already mentioned in my introduction, however, many readers of *To the Lighthouse* tend in their responses to Charles Tansley and Mr. Ramsay to replicate the feelings of hostility expressed by readers of *The Great Gatsby,* for example, who, following Nick's lead in this respect, think of Tom and Daisy Buchanan as unmitigated villains. Such responses arise from the fact that Woolf's narrator does—by mimicking the voices of characters who feel antagonistic toward them—present Charles Tansley and Mr. Ramsay in a way that arouses similar feelings in her readers, just as our other narrators had done before her. We should not, however, ignore the fact that Woolf, by using a narrator who is not bound by the limited vision of a particular character, ultimately deprives us of that satisfaction of our sacrificial passions for which she had seemingly prepared us.

ᘓ    ᘓ    ᘓ

The vision of relationships not grounded in sacrificial exclusion with which the novel concludes contrasts decisively, to be sure, with its opening scene. There, Woolf portrays James Ramsay as caught in a double bind whereby he wants to kill the father who, at the same time, he would like very much to emulate. Mr. Ramsay arrives with the unwelcome news that "it won't be fine" tomorrow (4), an eventuality for which he bears no personal responsibility. James, however, instinctively imputes a malign motivation to his father and wishes that he had at hand the means to destroy him: "Had there been an axe handy, or a poker, any weapon that would have gashed a hole in his father's breast and killed him, there and then, James would have seized it" (4). As Jane Lilienfeld has argued, James does not speak only for himself; rather, he "has been selected in this novel and by his family to voice inside himself the animosity attributed by narrative voices to all the Ramsay progeny" (192). The representative quality of James's attitude reveals, to be sure, the sacrificial implications of the violent thoughts that he directs toward his father, which are not simply a private matter between father and son.

The irony is that James strongly identifies with the father who has now become the target of his murderous thoughts, a point that Woolf makes clear in two related ways: through Mrs. Ramsay, who, picturing James as eventually assuming a public role similar to her husband's, "imagined him all red and ermine on the Bench or directing a stern and momentous enterprise in some crisis of public affairs" (4) and through James himself, whose instinctive desire to emulate his father is already inscribed in his demeanor: "he appeared the image of stark and uncompromising severity, with his high forehead and his fierce blue eyes, impeccably candid and pure, frowning slightly at the sight of human frailty" (4). James's violent feelings toward his father (whom he instinctively constructs as a scapegoat to replace the real antagonist of bad weather) are thus presented as inextricable from his desire, implicitly encouraged by his mother, to become his mirror image. This makes of Mr. Ramsay—in his son's eyes, as later in the eyes of Lily Briscoe—at once an admired model and a daunting obstacle who provokes resentful thoughts.

James's destructive passions are, however, aroused in "The Window," the section of *To the Lighthouse* that is governed by an underlying principle whereby male rivalry, and the emulative desires in which it originates, will not be allowed to lead to uncontrollable violence. Thus, after briefly displaying James's destructive passion, Woolf expels him to the periphery of her novel, replacing him with characters in whom the emulative impulse can be experienced without leading to a destructive scenario. Thus, we will shortly see Charles Tansley replacing James as he accompanies Mrs. Ramsay on her errands. Woolf alludes to the analogy between James and Tansley as aspirants to Mr. Ramsay's eminence by having Tansley wish Mrs. Ramsay "to see him, gowned and hooded, walking in a procession" (11). The effect produced on Tansley by the proximity of Mrs. Ramsay likewise mirrors the glow that she inspires in James: "for the first time in his life Charles Tansley felt an extraordinary pride; felt the wind and the cyclamen and the violets for he was walking with a beautiful woman. He had hold of her bag" (14). Unlike James, however, Tansley does not allow the joy that he experiences in Mrs. Ramsay's presence to lead to any murderous intent directed against her husband.

Similarly, in William Bankes, Woolf has created another potential rival: a lifelong friend of Mr. Ramsay's who could reasonably be expected to evince some envy with regard to the latter's good fortune in marrying such a beautiful woman and fathering such a flourishing brood of children. The narrator alludes to the potential grounds for rivalry in her remark that "Ramsay lived in a welter of children, whereas Bankes was childless and a widower" (21). Bankes himself, however, limits his expression of hostility to making sure that Lily Briscoe "should understand how things stood" between himself and Ramsay, by which he means that their friendship had petered out some years ago. So immune is Bankes to any feelings of aggressiveness toward a man who has everything that he could be imagined as wanting that he even goes so far as to insure "that Lily Briscoe should not disparage Ramsay" (21). Of all the characters in the novel, it is, to be sure, Lily Briscoe herself who must face in the most protracted and complex way the double bind that James briefly yet so dramatically illustrates in the novel's opening scene. Like James, she must learn how to gain access to a world of cultural achievements whose principal representative, Mr. Ramsay himself, arouses such powerful feelings of resentment and resistance.

Woolf likewise maintains the peaceful ambiance of "The Window" by allowing violent feelings to be safely directed, not against such an essential character as Mr. Ramsay, but toward such a clearly secondary and, thus, dispensable figure as Charles Tansley, whose modest social background, while not entirely excluding him from the Ramsay household, does decidedly distinguish him from its members. Tansley spares us the spectacle of parricidal rage or sibling rivalry among all eight of the Ramsay children by becoming himself the object of their aggression. Woolf underlines the unifying power of Tansley's otherness from the group by including even the family dog in the horde of Ramsays that descends upon him: "'The atheist,' they called him; 'the little atheist.' Rose mocked him; Prue mocked him; Andrew, Jasper, Roger mocked him; even old Badger without a tooth in his head bit him" (5-6). Unlike James, whom Woolf dismisses from "The Window" after he has served to remind us of the potentially destructive consequences of male rivalry, Charles Tansley plays the socially useful role of the figure who arouses the collective, unifying violence of the community as a whole.

The narrator will allude once again to the unifying power of the outsider toward the end of "The Window" when she pictures the guests at the dinner party as drawn together and, at least momentarily, welded into a community by the contrast between the candlelit room in which they are sitting and the darkness that begins on the other side of the windows. Woolf leaves no doubt that it is thanks to the expulsion of the darkness from the room that this group has been united: "Some change at once went through them all, as if this had really happened, and they were all conscious of making a party together in a hollow, on an island; had their *common cause* against that fluidity out there" (97; emphasis added). In this scene, Charles Tansley had earlier epitomized the potential for violent confrontation inherent in the rivalry between different social classes: "He scowled ahead of him. He could almost pity these mild cultivated people, who would be blown sky high, like bales of wool and barrels of apples, one of these days by the gunpowder that was in him" (91–92). Fortunately, however, the lighting of the candles, by uniting the group against the darkness outside, effectively defuses the destructive use of fire that Tansley had envisioned.

The description of the preparations for the dinner party—in particular, the making of the Boeuf en Daube—suggests that something resembling a sacrificial ritual, in which every gesture is prescribed by convention, is being reenacted: "Everything depended upon things being served up to the precise moment they were ready. The beef, the bay leaf, and the wine—all must be done to a turn. To keep it waiting was out of the question" (80). The "smell of burning" that Mrs. Ramsay detects at one point may remind us of an outcome that, while necessary to a sacrificial ritual, would have disastrous consequences for the sublimated sacrifice that is the dinner party.

Significantly, the success of this ritual depends upon the work of the outsiders who have made the Boeuf en Daube possible: Mildred, the hired cook who will prepare it, and the anonymous French cooks who perfected the recipe that she will use. The key role played by these outsiders in unifying the dinner guests is underlined by the narrator's remark that "they were having Mildred's masterpiece" (80) and by the guests' own tribute to France: "It is a French recipe of my grandmother's," said Mrs. Ramsay, speaking with a ring of great pleasure in her voice. Of course it was French. What passes for cookery in England is an abomination (they agreed)" (100–01). This special capacity of a French cultural achievement to inspire unity among Mrs. Ramsay's dinner guests had been curiously alluded to just a few moments earlier by the narrator's remark about a similar effect being produced by the speaking of the French language: "So, when there is a strife of tongues, at some meeting, the chairman, to obtain unity, suggests that every one shall speak in French. Perhaps it is bad French; French may not contain the words that express the speaker's thoughts; nevertheless speaking French imposes some order, some uniformity" (90).

Woolf conveys here the intuitive recognition that will make possible her eventual resolution of the otherwise insoluble conflict between the necessity of exclusion and her commitment to inclusion.

The discovery that the cultural achievements made possible by the boundary separating the French people from the English can, at the same time, pass back and forth over this boundary, thus permitting an English cook to reproduce a French masterpiece, sets the stage for Lily's eventual assimilation of the largely male (and French, as it happens) artistic tradition that will inspire her painting.

James Ramsay, like his father before him, will pass rather unproblematically into adulthood at the end of *To the Lighthouse* because, as a young man, he benefits from a ritual, symbolized by the passage of the tiller from father to son, that welcomes him into the fellowship of other male adventurers. For Lily Briscoe, who mirrors the experience of Cam Ramsay in this respect, no parallel ritual exists. Thus, throughout the novel, Woolf will underline the communal dimension of cultural activity in her portrayal of Mr. Ramsay's work while, in contrast, emphasizing Lily's isolation as she works on her painting.

Mr. Ramsay's involvement with a community of thinkers is made evident by the group of disciples who gather about him. He is, by implication, not the sole adventurer striving to reach "R." Likewise, he evaluates the results of his labors, and the prospects for their acquiring at least relative immortality, by measuring them against comparable achievements by other illustrious men, such as Sir Walter Scott and Shakespeare. He must also confront the possibility that his own work is an essentially futile and fruitless undertaking. Lily, on the other hand, develops her artistic craft in an apparent vacuum. While Mr. Ramsay is part of a tradition that readily acknowledges the importance of the work of one's predecessors, she is presented as either rebelling against or being ignorant of the models bequeathed to her by other painters. While everyone else seems to have fallen under the spell of Mr. Paunceforte's example, Lily is clearly allergic to the kind of paintings that he favors: "She would not have considered it honest to tamper with the bright violet and the staring white, since she saw them like that, fashionable though it was, since Mr. Paunceforte's visit, to see everything pale, elegant, semitransparent" (18–19).

Something more significant than her resistance to a particular painterly style is at stake, however, in her lack of acquaintance with the acknowledged masterpieces of western art. William Bankes wishes, in particular, that Lily could experience the elation that he had felt while visiting the great museums of Europe: "It would be a wonderful experience for her—the Sistine Chapel; Michel Angelo; and Padua with its Giottos" (71). When Lily remarks that exposure to greatness might only make one dissatisfied with one's own puny accomplishments, he responds by emphasizing, not the individual pride that one takes in a personal accomplishment, but the more diffuse satisfaction of contributing to an impersonal cultural undertaking: "We can't all be Titians and we can't all be Darwins, he said; at the same time he doubted whether you could have your Darwin or your Titian if it weren't for humble people like ourselves" (72).

Lily's painting is not, to be sure, without its antecedents. No painter would, looking at Mrs. Ramsay and James, spontaneously portray them as a "triangular purple shape" (52). The purple triangle owes as much to Lily's assimilation of the movement toward abstraction in modern painting as it does to any direct perception, however inspired or original.[5] The narrator, however, tends to downplay evidence of Lily's dependence on a community of painters. Consequently, her work appears to acquire an aura of radical individuality to which it has, in fact, no actual claim. This spurious attribution of originality leads the narrator to present Lily's painting as exclusively the product of her direct, unaided vision, rather than as an object that has been mediated by the artistic tradition to which she implicitly belongs.

Structurally, the absence of references to the artistic community whose existence has made Lily's achievement possible amounts to a compensatory "expulsion" whereby, not so much Mr. Ramsay himself, as the community of cultural workers that he epitomizes, and by which Lily feels herself to have been unjustly marginalized, may in its turn be consigned to a realm beyond the margins of the novel.[6] It is not until Lily—her confidence bolstered by a radically individualistic conception of artistic work—has brought her labors to a successful conclusion, that Woolf allows the positive role of the historical antagonist—here represented by Mr. Carmichael, who holds in his hand a *French* novel—to be fully acknowledged, not only with respect to Lily's work as a painter but to her own as a novelist. Woolf's borrowings in *To the Lighthouse* from the tradition of the French novel, like Lily's from the impressionist and postimpressionist movements, and Mildred's from the French culinary tradition, all serve as examples of the transgression of boundaries that lead to creative out-comes sharply at variance with the chaos that such transgressions will produce in "Time Passes."

An important current in Woolf criticism, abetted by Lily Briscoe's silence on the sources of her inspiration in the work of fellow painters, has attempted to associate Woolf's own achievement as a writer with the discovery, or the construction, of a radically distinct alternative tradition with its sources in the maternal.[7] Ellen Tremper's detailed argument that Lily's achievement essentially involves her learning to resolve the contradictory feelings that Mr. Ramsay provokes in her—and, thus, of her ability to relate in a sustaining and creative way to the patriarchal culture that he represents—is a useful corrective to this particular kind of misreading. At the same time, however, these misreadings, by reproducing the expulsion to which Lily herself subjects this culture, clarify the psychological need that it satisfies. They also help us to see the crucial structural function that Carmichael serves by implicitly representing the return of the artistic fellowship whose existence is otherwise repressed in the narration of Lily's achievement.

Several other critics have implied that the unexpected prominence granted to Mr. Carmichael in the novel's culminating scene (as well as his crucial placement at the beginning and end of "Time Passes") allows Woolf to stage the relationship between her novel and the inherited literary tradition upon which it depends. John Ferguson, for example, in "A Sea Change: Thomas de Quincy and Mr. Carmichael in *To the Lighthouse*," has argued that Carmichael is a fictional representation of DeQuincey, a writer for whom Woolf expressed admiration on several occasions and whose stylistic innovations are an important source of her own. In "The Earth of Our Earliest Life," Ellen Tremper, after disputing this identification of Carmichael with DeQuincey, suggests that Carmichael's attachment to the poetry of Virgil provides a more significant key to our understanding of his role in the novel. She argues, in particular, that Virgil's emphasis on the necessity of the human struggle against nature provides the background to the individual struggle undertaken, especially in "The Lighthouse" section, by Lily. J. Hillis Miller, while not identifying Carmichael with a historical model, does connect his poeticizing reverie with the narrative technique that Woolf adopted for the novel as a whole. For Miller, Carmichael's subjective point of view, which we are rarely shown directly, is felt everywhere in the stylistic features of the novel.

These critics do not, however, explain the disproportion between the great importance that they ascribe to the cultural tradition represented by Carmichael and the limited presence, amounting to his virtual marginalization, that Woolf actually allots to him in the novel. The critics who mistakenly laud Lily's achievement for its radical originality as well as for its revolutionary assault on "patriarchal" aesthetic and social conventions, are much closer, in spite of their crucial misreading of this point, to the ambivalence—that mixture of admiration and resentment provoked in its most dramatic form by Mr. Ramsay—that Woolf resolves through the expedient of largely dismissing allusions to the communal aspects of cultural labor in her account of Lily's struggle to affirm her own individuality within this tradition.

In the "Time Passes" section, the outsiders who unite the community—either by channeling its aggressive impulses outside of the group or by creating cultural objects that can be enjoyed by the community as a whole—suddenly disappear. The darkness against which the dinner guests had successfully waged their "common cause" and the Boeuf en Daube that they had consumed in common, are no longer available for the ritual purposes that they had served in "The Window." The threat of chaos that had once been embodied in a moderated, controllable, and even occasionally lovable form in the person of Mr. Ramsay can no longer be displaced upon a designated figure: Charles Tansley disappears entirely and Mr. Ramsay makes only a brief—and merely parenthetical—appearance. Consequently, the threat of chaos that had been providentially averted throughout the first section of the novel will now be allowed to reach virtually cosmic proportions. Whereas in "The Window" the antagonism represented by the threat of bad weather had been transferred to Mr. Ramsay's "tempestuous" presence, the process of personification is now reversed: in place of human characters who are made to bear the burden of cosmic disturbances, we find a natural world that has acquired human characteristics. Thus, we learn that "[n]othing, it seemed, could survive the flood, the profusion of darkness which, creeping in at keyholes and crevices, stole round window blinds, came into bedrooms, swallowed up here a jug and basin, there a bowl of red and yellow dahlias, there the sharp edges and firm bulk of a chest of drawers" (125–26). The wind is similarly described as "send[ing] its spies" and the weeds as "tapp[ing] methodicaly at the window-pane" (132). The "gigantic chaos" that descends upon the Ramsays' house will be humanized as a "tumbling and tossing" figure (134).

Since the darkness acquired its unifying power at the time of the dinner party thanks to the lighting of the candles, it is entirely appropriate that it should lose this power precisely at the moment when the lamps within the Ramsays' house are extinguished. The significance of the gradual extinction of these lights becomes clearer when we consider the revisions that Woolf introduced into this part of her novel. As James M. Haule has pointed out, in "*To the Lighthouse* and the Great War: The Evidence of Virginia Woolf's Revisions of 'Time Passes,'" the original holograph of the "Time Passes" section tended, rather, to attribute its pervasive violence to male aggressiveness. He also notes that Woolf had initially characterized Mrs. McNab in such a way as to create a clear-cut opposition between male destructiveness and female creativity: "In the holograph, the principle opposed to the female restorer of hope, order, and forgiveness is overtly male and sexually threatening" (in Hussey, *Woolf and War,* 171). Haule concludes that of the many changes that Woolf made between the holograph and the finished version of this section," perhaps the most dramatic is the extent to which Woolf altered the anti-male aggressor and antiwar focus of this pivotal section" (166).

Haule recognizes that Woolf's removal of details that create this pattern of male/female opposition shifts the emphasis of this section from the particular to the universal" (177) without, however, explaining satisfactorily how this effect is achieved. As he correctly observes, the holograph version expresses "a feminist's view of the violence of war, which she associates with male sexual brutality" (166). He attributes Woolf's alterations to the fact that, while she "was contemptuous of self-serving male interpretations . . . [s]he was equally reluctant, however, to give full vent to her own radical opinion, not because it was unpopular or because she lacked courage but because it was not the 'history' she wanted to write and, however appealing, it was not art" (167). According to Haule, Woolf's reluctance led her, regrettably, to produce a final version of the section that is "without the anti-militaristic, fiercely feminist condemnation of the pointless violence of blind male dominion" (173).

Haule suggests, in effect, that Woolf sacrificed truth to the requirements of art by producing in "Time Passes" a version of history that was at variance with history as she truly saw it. An alternative explanation—which credits Woolf with approaching even more closely to the truth of history at the same time that she deepened the art of her novel—is that, as she revised "Time Passes," she moved away from the comparatively superficial view that attributes war to male violence and toward the more complex recognition of the role played by the disappearance of firmly maintained distinctions. Thus, Woolf may be credited with intuitively expressing in *To the Lighthouse* a vision that goes much deeper than the presumably more "feminist" view contained in the holograph version.

In another study of Woolf's revisions, entitled "'Le Temps Passe' and the Original Typescript," Haule indirectly supports this conclusion when he observes that the typescript of the "Time Passes" section begins with darkness . . . not with the gradual extinction of light. . . . The typescript begins with no mention of specific character and no hint of light" (271). The earlier version begins with the process of encroaching darkness, unrelated to any prior cause, already well underway: "It grew darker. Clouds covered the moon; in the early hours of the morning a thin rain drummed on the roof, and starlight and moonlight and all light on sky and earth was quenched" (279). The revised version, however, specifically attributes the encroaching darkness—and the resurgence of a violent, undifferentiated world that it represents—to the disappearance of something that had until then remained distinct from the darkness, that is, the lamps that had been kept lit within the house:

> "Do we leave that light burning?" said Lily as they took their coats off indoors.
> "No," said Prue, "not if every one's in."
> "Andrew, she called back, 'just put out the light in the hall."
> One by one the lamps were extinguished, except that Mr. Carmichael, who liked to lie awake a little reading Virgil, kept his candle burning rather longer than the rest.

Thus concludes the first chapter of this section; the second chapter then begins with:

> So with the lamps all put out, the moon sunk, and a thin rain drumming on the roof a downpouring of immense darkness began. Nothing, it seemed, could survive the flood, the profusion of darkness which, creeping in at keyholes and crevices, stole round window blinds, came into bedrooms, swallowed up here a jug and basin, there a bowl of red and yellow dahlias, there the sharp edges and firm bulk of a chest of drawers. (125–26)

Light and darkness no longer play the mutually self-defining roles that had given at least some minimal shape to the night, a point that Woolf further emphasizes a moment later when she allows the process of disintegration to move to an even further stage when "Mr. Carmichael, who was reading Virgil, blew out his candle" (127). These revisions of "Time Passes," suggest that the potential for chaos inherent in male violence, which had been successfully contained and channeled in "The Window," is finally activated by the absence of a figure (corresponding to a solitary lamp) sufficiently different from the community to have produced in it a unifying "common cause." It is as though Tansley's fantasy of blowing his dinner companions "sky high," which is allowed only parenthetical mention at the dinner party thanks to the lighting of the candles, now achieves its fulfillment with the extinguishing of the various lamps that had until now distinguished the house from the darkness.

The dissolution of boundaries, which itself portends the return of the chaos that had been kept in the novel's margins by a firmly established exclusionary procedure, is alluded to in the opening page of this section when, as night descends, Prue observes that "[o]ne can hardly tell which is the sea and which is the land" (125). The darkness that had, during the dinner party, reliably fulfilled its role as the embodiment of what must be excluded in order that the stability of the community be maintained, now becomes uncontrollably invasive: "So with lamps all put out, the moon sunk, and a thin rain drumming on the roof a downpouring of immense darkness began" (125). The pattern whereby reciprocal differences lose their grounding in reality—which begins with the confusion between the land

and the sea—then reappears in the weakening of sexual difference: "Not only was the furniture confounded; there was scarcely anything left of body or mind by which one could say, 'This is he' or 'This is she'" (126). In a metaphor that alludes to World War I, Woolf mirrors this confusion of sexual identity in the uncertain distinction that she now establishes between friend and foe: "Were they allies? Were they enemies?" (126). Additional forms of merging are then suggested by the narrator's remark that "night and day, month and year ran shapelessly together" (134).

This process, which begins with the blurring of the boundary between land and sea, and proceeds to dissolve the difference between "he" and "she" and between "ally" and "adversary," culminates in the collapse of the distinction between the human and the non-human. For this reason, one of the most memorable scenes in the novel—in which the natural world begins to reclaim the untended summer house of the Ramsays—is not so much a historical event as it is a phenomenon that illustrates the timeless threat of reversion to primordial chaos, an eventuality that Woolf will intuitively cast in language that evokes the return of male rivalry: "it seemed as if the universe were battling and tumbling, in brute confusion and wanton lust aimlessly by itself" (135).

The parallel that this metaphor establishes between purely natural forms of chaos and those that are specifically provoked by human agents will also emerge in Woolf's description of the house's deterioration. In part, this is a purely natural occurrence: "the garden was a pitiful sight now, all run to riot, and the rabbits scuttling at you out of the beds" (136) and "[t]oads had nosed their way in [to the house]" (137). Along with these purely natural forms of "invasion," however, the narrator also envisions the arrival of human visitors who ignore the rights of the Ramsays as the owners of the house:

> In the ruined room, picnickers would have lit their kettles; lovers sought shelter there, lying on the bare boards; and the shepherd stored his dinner on the bricks, and the tramp slept with his coat round him to ward off the cold. Then the roof would have fallen; briars and hemlocks would have blotted out path, step and window; would have grown, unequally but lustily over the mound, until some trespasser, losing his way, could have told only by a red-hot poker among the nettles, or

a scrap of china in the hemlock that here once someone had lived; there had been a house. (138–39)

The arrival of this caravan of trespassers is an ironic rewriting of the dinner party in which the original, orderly lowering of the barrier between the family and its guests is now reproduced in a totally chaotic way. This imagined scene thus parallels the dinner party presented in "The Window," in such a way, however, as to remind us that the success of the earlier scene depended on the exclusion of outsiders—symbolically represented by the darkness—which now return in myriad and uncontrollable forms.

Since the disappearance of a stable boundary had precipitated the return of unbounded disorder in "Time Passes," it is not surprising that the restoration of order with which this section concludes will be initiated by its reappearance. Thus, Woolf assigns the task of preparing the house for the Ramsays' return to two lower-class women, Mrs. McNab and Mrs. Bast, just as she had attributed the creation of the "masterpiece" of Boeuf en Daube to Mildred, the Ramsays' cook. As James M. Haule has pointed out, the holograph of this section clearly shows that Woolf originally imagined Mrs. McNab as an archetypal figure, "an ancient female symbol of life and regeneration" (Hussey, *Virginia Woolf and War,* 170). He observes, however, that subsequent revisions radically altered this initial image, to the extent that he will say of the Mrs. McNab that we actually meet toward the end of "Time Passes," "[t]he regeneration of the earth is no longer the mission of an ancient female of near poetic intelligence. She is *just a maid* who performs her duties without reflection" (172; emphasis added).

This revised image of the Ramsays' maids is clearly in evidence when the narrator describes Mrs. McNab and Mrs. Bast as "a force working; something not highly conscious; something that leered, something that lurched" (139), a description in which we sense the implicit, yet firmly maintained, distance between the genteel narrator and her uncultured laborers. She then goes on to attribute to them a cluster of personal characteristics that further mark them as not belonging to the same social class as the Ramsays. Mrs. McNab, for example, is described as a "toothless, bonneted, care-taking woman" (130), whose walk is an "amble and hobble" (131). The narrator likewise imagines that her principal experiences of happiness must have occurred "at the wash-tub" or "at the public-house" (131), her favorite activities being drinking and gossiping. She also attributes syntactically dubious turns of speech both to Mrs. McNab, who complains that "[p]rices had gone up shamefully, and didn't come down again neither" (136) and to Mrs. Bast, who wonders "[w]hatever they [the Ramsays] hung that beast's skull there for" (140). Such linguistic derelictions would, presumably, never have been welcomed at the Ramsays' dinner table.

The narrator underlines this point when she has Mrs. McNab remember being a spectator to a dinner party that she had glimpsed only from an appropriate distance: "she had seen them once through the dining-room door. Twenty she dared say all in their jewelry, and she asked to stay help wash up, might be till after midnight" (140). She has, by way of compensation, more vivid memories of Mildred the cook than any of the dinner guests were likely to have had: "There was the cook now, Mildred, Marian, some such name as that—a red-headed woman, quick tempered like all her sort, but kind too, if you knew the way with her. Many a laugh they had had together. She saved a plate of soup for Maggie; a bite of ham, sometimes; whatever was over" (140).

All of these details—underlining as they do the nearly compete lack of resemblance between the cleaning ladies on the one hand and the Ramsays and their guests on the other—identify Mrs. McNab and Mrs. Bast as precisely the outsiders needed to transform the disorder that began entering the Ramsays' home with the extinguishing of the lamps. Thus, the members of the household, who had earlier drawn their stability from, in turn, Mrs. Ramsay's beauty, Mr. Ramsay's genius, Charles Tansley's odiousness, and the fluid darkness against which its members wage their "common cause," will now be sustained by the labors of Mrs. McNab and Mrs. Bast who, like Mildred, as well as the French cooks who made her masterpiece possible, will always to some extent remain outside of the community that their activity has brought into existence.

The process of displacing blame for the intractable problems of life itself upon a designated scapegoat, which we observed in James's construction of his father as an unmitigated villain, recurs at the beginning of "The Lighthouse." Having sufficiently characterized Mr. Ramsay as a "tempestuous" figure in "The Window"—and having, furthermore, contrived to keep him alive in "The Lighthouse" even though Sir Leslie Stephen (Woolf's father and the model of Mr. Ramsay) had died long before World War I—Woolf then shows Lily Briscoe casting him in the role of the scapegoat:

> But with Mr. Ramsay bearing down on her [Lily Briscoe], she could do nothing. Every time he approached—he was walking up and down the terrace—ruin approached, chaos approached. She could not paint. She stooped, she turned; she took up this rag; she squeezed that tube. But all she did was to ward him off a moment. He made it impossible for her to do anything. (148)

Mr. Ramsay produces precisely the paralyzing effect that Lily feared she would experience by encountering the work of the great masters in the museums of Europe. It is not, to be sure, the reaction that he provokes in other characters in the novel. His wife has high praise for him and the young men who admire his genius are drawn voluntarily to his company rather than fleeing his approach. The characters who do experience his approach as precipitating chaos are those who are not yet sure of their ability to meet the cultural standards that he embodies: these include his son James, who resents in him a power that he has not yet entirely acquired for himself, and Lily Briscoe, who wants to become like him by pursuing her own cultural project rather than consenting to serve as midwife to his. To recall the military metaphors of the "Time Passes" section, they are characters who have not yet achieved an accommodation that would permit them to live in peace with a neighbor who, in the absence of an agreed-upon "common cause," has become a potentially dangerous adversary. Fortunately, the threat of incipient chaos that Lily experiences here—which is allowed to reach genuinely uncontrollable proportions in "Time Passes"—will, in "The Lighthouse," be successfully contained by the "sacrificial" departure of Mr. Ramsay.

The final section of *To the Lighthouse* illustrates the process whereby a human community that is threatened by the resurgence of reciprocal violence protects itself against this eventuality by reestablishing an exclusionary ritual. Charles Tansley has not returned to vacation with the remaining Ramsays; thus, Mr. Ramsay

must assume his mantle as the chief object of hostility. Lily will ac-
cuse him of "never giving" (149) and of being "a lion seeking whom
he could devour" (156). The validity of these accusations is less important than their structural function of legitimizing his eventual
exclusion and associating it with plausible benefits to Lily. Like the
scapegoat in a sacrificial ritual, he must be identified as the source
of Lily's troubles in order that his expulsion be perceived as an effi-
cacious act.

The expulsion itself will occur in two phases. First, the expedition
to the lighthouse will effectively remove Mr. Ramsay from Lily's presence. The journey itself no longer possesses the narrative urgency
with which Mrs. Ramsay had imbued it when she vividly portrayed
the precarious circumstances of the lighthouse-keeper's life. Its new
purpose is to distance Mr. Ramsay from Lily Briscoe so that she may
complete her painting in the comparatively untroubling company of
Augustus Carmichael. Thus, as soon as the expedition is launched,
Lily returns to her painting, which now, curiously, acquires attributes
that recall Mr. Ramsay to mind, but in a more moderate and man-
ageable way:

> She saw her canvas as if it had floated up and placed itself
> white and uncompromising directly before her. It seemed to
> rebuke her with its cold stare for all this hurry and agitation;
> this folly and waste of emotion; it drastically recalled her and
> spread through her mind first a peace, as her disorderly sen-
> sations (he had gone and she had been so sorry for him and
> she had said nothing) trooped off the field; and then, empti-
> ness. She looked blankly at the canvas, *with its uncompromising*
> *white stare;* from the canvas to the garden. (156–57; emphasis
> added)

Mr. Ramsay's imperious gaze, which we first saw in emulated form on
James Ramsay's face, has now migrated to Lily's canvas. Woolf uses
this displacement to emphasize the substitutive role of the painting,
which then allows Lily to resolve her conflict with Mr. Ramsay, not by
resorting to the kind of violence that James Ramsay had contemplated in the novel's opening scene, but by struggling to achieve a
place in the realm of cultural activity that he represents. The per-
sonified canvas, while severe and capable of judging her work a fail-

ure, presents her with aesthetic demands that she can potentially satisfy.[8] Thus, while the struggle to meet the requirements of the painting "often brought her to the verge of tears," it also provides her with the occasion to struggle "against terrific odds to maintain her courage" (10). As Ellen Tremper has pointed out, in her essay, "In Her Father's House: *To the Lighthouse* as a Record of Virginia Woolf's Literary Patrimony," the vocabulary of heroic endeavor that Woolf adopts to describe the challenge that Lily faces implicitly shows her becoming a self—neither woman nor child—"that feels and thinks in his [Mr. Ramsay's] conventionally masculine terms" (10). At the same time, her success in completing this quest depends, to be sure, on Mr. Ramsay himself continuing on his way to the lighthouse rather than encroaching upon Lily's personal space in his actual person.

Having helped to create the necessary distance between Mr. Ramsay and Lily, the boat now becomes the setting for an additional exclusionary act in which Cam and James will bond together by directing their feelings of hostility toward their father: "But they vowed, in silence, as they walked, to stand by each other and carry out the great compact—to resist tyranny to the death" (163). Hermione Lee has usefully observed that the sacrificial aspect of this scene is given further dimension by "the throwing back of the magical flounder [which] might suggest the fish with a piece cut out of it, thrown into the sea on the voyage to the lighthouse like a sacrificial offering" (in Bloom, *Virginia Woolf's "To the Lighthouse,"* 18).

At the same time that Woolf allows Mr. Ramsay to become the object of his children's aggressive feelings, however, she also creates an opposing image that contests the caricature that they have made of him. Thus Cam, while accusing her father of having poisoned her childhood, recognizes nevertheless that "no one attracted her more; his hands were beautiful, and his feet, and his voice, and his words, and his haste, and his temper, and his oddity, and his passion, and his saying straight out before every one, we perish, each alone, and his remoteness" (169). Later, recalling the image of her father writing in his study, she realizes that "he was not vain, nor a tyrant and did not wish to make you pity him. Indeed, if he saw she was there, reading a book, he would ask her, as gently as anyone could, Was there nothing he could give her?" (189–90).

Similarly, James, who defines tyranny rather broadly as "making people do what they did not want to do" (184), had thought at one moment to "take a knife and strike him [Mr. Ramsay] to his heart" (184). He nonetheless recognizes that his real problem is not with his father but with a quasi-demonic figure—doubtlessly a personification of his own rivalistic impulses—that tempts him to an irrational act of violence: "It was the thing that descended on him— without his knowing it perhaps: that fierce sudden black-winged harpy, with its talons and its beak all cold and hard, that struck and struck at you (he could feel the beak on his bare legs, where it had struck when he was a child) and then made off" (184).

Like her husband, Mrs. Ramsay—to whom Lily had recurrently attached blame throughout "The Window" for her obsession with marriage—will now become the object of a process of rehabilitation. Her death in "Time Passes" has the emotional effect of a sacrificial act that liberates Lily from the paralyzing expectations that she had epitomized for her. For this reason, there is no necessity, in her case, of arranging for the process of exclusion to which Mr. Ramsay is subjected. For Lily the problem is, rather. the contrary: how to revive an image of Mrs. Ramsay that is sufficiently vivid to provide her with the inspiration that she needs in order to complete her painting. Thus, the Mrs. Ramsay whom Lily—imitating, in this respect, James's behavior toward his father—vows to resist during the dinner party, now becomes the object of an invocation designed to retrieve her from the realm of the dead. Lily will, to be sure, preserve elements of her earlier animosity toward Mrs. Ramsay, as we see in the pleasure that she takes in reflecting on the fact that relationships between various characters have not developed as Mrs. Ramsay would have wished (175). But this exorcism of Mrs. Ramsay in the form of an imagined triumph over her conforms to that softening of sacrificial impulses that characterizes "The Lighthouse," as is shown by Lily's opposing effort to maintain her bond with her mentor: "If they shouted loud enough Mrs. Ramsay would return. 'Mrs. Ramsay!' she said aloud, 'Mrs. Ramsay!' The tears ran down her face" (180).

Yet another example of the rehabilitation of a sacrificial figure involves Charles Tansley who, while physically absent from "The Lighthouse" conveniently returns in Lily's memory to resume his role as the most easily attacked of the novel's outsiders. Resorting to an impersonal formula that implies the existence of an entire community that dislikes Tansley, Lily reflects that "[I]t was part of the reason why one disliked him. He upset the proportions of one's world" (196). She disparages him for trying to preach brotherly love but succeeding only in "pumping love into that chilly space" (197). Finally, however, Lily has a revelation that permits her to recognize the degree to which she has unjustly turned Tansley into a scapegoat:

> Her own idea of him was grotesque, Lily knew well, stirring the plantains with her brush. Half one's notions of other people were, after all, grotesque. They served private purposes of one's own. He did for her instead of a whipping-boy. She found herself flagellating his lean flanks when she was out of temper. If she wanted to be serious about him she had to help herself to Mrs. Ramsay's sayings, to look at him through her eyes. (197)

"The Lighthouse" begins, then, with a threat of chaos that is warded off by successive exclusionary acts that are, in their turn, repudiated by the three chief perpetrators of this atavistic ritual: Cam, James, and Lily Briscoe. In a final phase Woolf points to the possibility of creating forms of social order in which the practice of scapegoating—whose target is now recognized as the victim of an unjust exclusion—has been significantly moderated. Whereas Cam Ramsay will be excluded from the act of cultural transmission through which Mr. Ramsay bestows the tiller on her brother James, Lily Briscoe will, on the contrary, enter the cultural realm by mirroring the cultural activity of her fellow artist Augustus Carmichael, who witnesses her achievement, rather than proclaiming its impossibility.[9]

Woolf organizes the double ending of the novel—the arrival of the family at the lighthouse and the completion of Lily's painting—in such a way as to imply an underlying parallel between the two processes. However, there is also a fundamental asymmetry between the two conclusions. James's achievement is the more traditional of the two and so receives less extensive treatment. Essentially, he gains recognition in the eyes of his father by performing an act (guiding the boat to the lighthouse) that has until now been associated with Mr. Ramsay. Lily, however, faces the more complicated challenge of successfully crossing gender lines by gaining recognition from the resuscitated figure of Mrs. Ramsay while engaging in a form of cultural activity that has been gendered throughout the novel as exclusively male.

In the simpler, traditional version of the process that is reenacted on the boat there is no question as to the identity of the child to whom Mr. Ramsay will entrust the tiller. It must be surrendered to James because it was he who had dreamed of killing his father "[had] there been an axe handy, or a poker" (4). The tiller symbolizes the peaceful, and culturally useful, means for resolving the potentially murderous struggle alluded to by James's spontaneous, natural resort to lethal weapons. Back on the shore, however, Woolf considerably revises this process. In this final scene, the formation of a fellowship that implies the loss of distinction between "he" and "she"—which in "Time Passes" had contributed to the reversion to chaotic violence—now represents the possibility of a non-exclusionary relationship with the other.

As we had noticed earlier, Woolf stages Lily's actual work on her painting in such a way as to suppress allusions to the male artists from whom she has drawn her inspiration. In this way, she creates a mirror image of the exclusionary ritual that takes place in the boat: the father and son who bonded by excluding Cam as they arrived at the lighthouse are now excluded in their turn from the bond that draws Lily and Mrs. Ramsay together as Lily moves toward the completion of her painting. Once the painting has been completed, however, Woolf allows us to see that the exclusion that made it possible was only a temporizing strategy to which she attaches no permanent significance.

James Ramsay had to be excluded from the novel after its opening scene in order that the serenity of "The Window" not be threatened by his incipient rivalry with his father. The working-class characters likewise disappear from the novel rather than obtaining entry into the world of cultural achievement that their labor has made possible. Cam Ramsay protests only to herself against the collusion between her father and her brother that has led to her exclusion. Lily's artistic achievement, however, points to the fact that, ultimately at least, the fellowship of cultural activity is equally the province of those whom, like James Ramsay, it has traditionally welcomed and those whom, like Lily Briscoe, it has excluded.

# Notes

## INTRODUCTION:
## FROM RITUAL TO MODERNISM

1. The solitude of its heroes and the presence of mythic resonances have long been recognized as hallmarks of modernist literature. For excellent recent discussions of these related features see Edward Engelberg's *Solitude and Its Ambiguities in Modernist Fiction* and Michael Bell's *Literature, Modernism and Myth: Belief and Responsibility in the Twentieth Century*.

2. The Freudian interest in the psychology of the isolated protagonist has had a far greater influence on interpretations of modernist novels than Girard's concern with the sacrificial implications of this same figure. Paula Cohen's essay on *The Turn of the Screw* in relation to Freud's *The Case of Dora* is a good example of the fruitfulness of this approach, as is Edmund Wilson's classic Freudian analysis of the governess's sexual frustrations. Both Catherine Rising's "Conrad and Kohut: The Fortunate Oedipal Fall" and Barbara Johnson and Marjorie Garber's "Secret Sharing: Reading Conrad Psychoanalytically" testify to the enduring appeal of the Freudian approach. Giles Mitchell's debunking of Gatsby in "The Great Narcissist: A Study of Fitzgerald's *The Great Gatsby* is similarly indebted to Freud, as is Ami Krumrey's article, "Nick Carraway's Process of Individuation," which appeared in the *Journal of Evolutionary Psychology*. The tendency of critics, following Freud's lead, to invoke *Oedipus the King* while entirely overlooking the play's sacrificial implications may be observed in Bruce Bassoff's insightful essay, "Oedipal Fantasy and Arrested Development in *The Good Soldier*." In Woolf studies, the vitality of Freudian readings is evident in such essays as Diana Swanson's "An Antigone Complex? Psychology and Politics in *The Years* and *Three Guineas*," Dorothy Robbins' "Virginia Woolf and Sigmund Freud Diverge on What a Woman Wants," and Judith Lutzer's "Woolf and Freud: An Analysis of Invisible Presences."

3. For useful analyses of these modernist works in relation to sacrificial rituals, see John Vickery's chapter, "James Joyce: *Ulysses* and the Human scapegoat," in his *The Literary Impact of "The Golden Bough"* and Matthew Krattner's discussions of *The Waste Land* and *Light in August* in his "Christ Follows Dionysus."

4. One of the most interesting studies of the strategies used by modernist writers to satisfy their craving for order and, in this way, to protect themselves from the fear of psychic disintegration is John J. Clayton's *Gestures of Healing: Anxiety and the Modern Novel*. Clayton argues that modernism is "shaped by common pain from a common source and from various attempts to cope with pain—gestures of healing—reparative acts that permit writers to feel whole and to make some link, other than alienation, with the world. These attempts are, I think, only gestures. They express longing for wholeness, they point to the place of wholeness even though they cannot make the artist whole. Or if they can, it is only temporarily: the pain has to be assuaged over and over, the broken places knitted again and again" (4). Clayton does not, however, pursue the analogy between this individual quest for order and the communal creation of order through sacrificial rituals that is also echoed throughout modernist texts. His discussion of the "aesthetics of order" that characterizes modernist fiction nonetheless contributes invaluably to our understanding of how modernist authors attempt to create order without resorting to such rituals.

5. In this respect the novels chosen for this study reenact the tension found already in the gospels, which, as Girard notes, lend themselves to a *mythic* reading, in which the Jews are targeted as replacement scapegoats in a manner that is clearly at variance with the conscious attitude of rejection of scapegoating exemplified by the proclamation of Christ as the innocent victim. (See *Things Hidden Since the Foundation of the World*, 257, 264, and 265.)

6. All page numbers cited in the text are to Henry James, *The Aspern Papers and The Turn of the Screw* (New York: Penguin, 1985).

7. All page numbers cited in the text are to Joseph Conrad, *Heart of Darkness* (New York: Penguin, 1995).

8. All page numbers cited in the text are to Ford Madox Ford, *The Good Soldier* (New York: Vintage Books, 1989).

9. All pages cited in the text are to F. Scott Fitzgerald, *The Great Gatsby* (New York: Scribner, 1995).

10. All page numbers cited in the text are to Virginia Woolf, *To the Lighthouse* (New York: Harcourt Brace Jovanovich, 1981).

11. Adopting a perspective similar to my own, Gary Watson, in his analysis of D. H. Lawrence's novella, *The Virgin and the Gypsy*, calls attention to the fact that Yvette's grandmother becomes an alternative scapegoat whose sacrificial expulsion is generally unperceived by readers because the narrator succeeds in making her unredeemably repugnant and because her actual death is accomplished thanks to the deus ex machina device of the flood in which she drowns. His remark that the readers of the novella are invited to play the role of the "mob" that consents to ritual murder is relevant to the similar way in which the novels that I have chosen for this study construct their readers. His concluding observation—to the effect that the novella itself argues that "René Girard may be wrong to think that effective scapegoating is becoming increasingly more difficult to bring off in the modern world. What Lawrence shows us is that it *can* be done and it can be done virtually in the open" ("Fact and Significance of Desire," 154)—is invaluable.

## CHAPTER 1.
## OCCULTED RIVALRY IN *THE TURN OF THE SCREW*

1. Several recent analyses of *The Turn of the Screw* have given an additional dimension to James's allusion to communal persecutions by finding in contemporaneous "witch trials"—especially those involving the pursuit of homosexuals, which culminated in the trial of Oscar Wilde—a crucial subtext to James's novel. According to Eric Haralson, James is known to have been revolted by the circumstances of Wilde's trial and imprisonment, which he referred to as a chapter of "hideous human history" (quoted in McCormack, *Questioning the Master*, 140). Haralson deduces from the Wildean subtext of the novel that it is "No surprise, then, that the tale begins with a character named Douglas (as in Lord Alfred) and culminates in a tribunal and humiliation ritual à la Oscar Wilde's, with the governess simulating a prosecutorial force" (ibid.).

2. See Jeff Williams's analysis of the frame tale in terms of the "one-upmanship" that clearly motivates Douglas's decision to tell his story to the assembled company. For Williams, the frame tale essentially "depicts the performance of *competing narratives*. Douglas's motive is explicitly to outdo Griffin" ("Narrative Games," 49). He concludes, rightly I believe, that the primary link between the frame tale and the main story rests with the common factor of "enthrallment": the governess's narrative will, like Douglas's performance, be motivated by the desire to produce a certain emotional effect in its listeners. For this reason, Williams argues, the criterion by which her account should be judged is not the realistic one of accuracy (which most critics have wrongly emphasized) but, rather, its rhetorical effectiveness.

In Williams's view, the only relevant question is whether or not the governess has succeeded in fashioning a story capable, as it were, of holding its audience "breathless." He does not, however, pursue an obvious implication of this insight: if the governess is like Douglas in presenting to her readers an "enthralling" narrative then perhaps she is also like him in competing with an impressive predecessor. "Who, then, is *her* 'Griffin,'" we may ask. We may also wonder whether James hinted at the answer to this question (i.e., "the *ghosts* of Peter Quint and Miss Jessel") by giving to Douglas's storytelling predecessor the name "Griffin," which, like the word "ghosts," designates a mythical creature. I will also argue that—although the governess's narrative is, as Williams would argue, best read as a public performance (one that employs certain rhetorical strategies whose purpose is to provoke a precise emotional response in her audience)—we, as readers, are called upon, not simply to register her success or failure in producing this response but to question the ethical implications of her performance.

3. See E. C. Curtsinger's discussion of the novella as an allegory of the creative process. According to Curtsinger, the narrator, Douglas, and the governess represent, respectively, the head, heart, and the imagination as each contributes to the creative process (352). Peter Quint, in contrast, represents the forces of "anti-creation" ("Turn of the Screw as Writer's parable," 357). The chief defect of this interpretation is that, by insisting so exclusively on the allegorical significance of

characters, it ignores their real-life relationships, and the personal conflicts (including rivalry) that these involve. It does, however, have the singular merit of recognizing that the frame tale presents in a cooperative and successful way a process that had led to a tragic outcome in the main story.

4. See, for example, Millicent Bell (in Ian Bell, *Henry James,* 100) and Alice Hall Petry ("Jamesian Parody," 76) on *Jayne Eyre* as a model.

5. The readiness of critics to impute evil motivations to the ghosts may be noted even in the interpretation offered by so astute a critic as Millicent Bell, for whom Miss Jessel is the projection of a malign aspect of the governess herself. In the course of her subsequent analysis, Bell maintains that Quint is an evil character (in Ian Bell, *Henry James,* 104) as well as a "nightmarish" figure (115), and that Miss Jessel has transgressed sexual boundaries (106). Daniel R. Schwartz, speculating at one point that "Quint seems to be a pederast" (14), suggests that the ghosts have introduced the children to homosexuality. More than anything, this interpretation reveals just how difficult it is for a reader to contemplate the possibility that Miss Jessel, like the governess, may want nothing more than to *be at Bly.*

6. Millicent Bell has pointed to the fact that the "governess novel," a popular literary form at the time, promoted to primary rank a figure that had until then played a merely secondary role (in Ian Bell, *Henry James,* 95). From this perspective, we could say that the form of *The Turn of the Screw* itself mirrors, or serves to fulfill, the ambitions of its narrator.

7. Susan Crowl recognizes that the governess's seemingly "deeply private experience" is also a "social gesture." However, she means by this only that the "literary" act whereby such public elements of her narrative as Bly itself and the events that occur there become metaphors for her personal experience. She does not recognize that this personal experience has, already, a public, prosecutorial dimension.

8. Along with Leon Edel, Eric Haralson is an important exception to this rule, although his focus on a homosexual subplot may be unduly narrowing. Haralson argues that the "governess is the mere (murderous) handmaiden of patriarchy," whose behavior reminds us of "the heavy sacrifice that British society stood ready to incur to prevent 'little gentlemen' like him [Miles] from straying into 'the wrong path altogether'" (in McCormack, *Questioning the Master,* 139). This contention leads Haralson to raise a question that has an important bearing on my own argument: ". . . what if Miles's nominal crime—incipient same-sex desire—were grasped as purely a cultural fabrication, rather than a theological 'evil' or a pathological 'deviance?' How on earth would one then judge his executioner?" (147). In a similar vein, Millicent Bell has pointed out that a governess, by definition, speaks not only in her own name but as the defender of public morality.

9. Shoshana Felman overlooks this point in her otherwise brilliant analysis of the novella's way of alternatively arousing and frustrating our desire to capture its meaning: "And what James in effect *does* in *The Turn of the Screw,* what he undertakes through the performative action of his text, is precisely to mislead us, and to catch us, by on the contrary inviting us to catch the unconscious in the act" (in Esch and Warren, *Turn of the Screw,* 222). Her subsequent, psychologizing designa-

tion of Miles as representing "unmasterable unconscious knowledge," although doubtlessly insightful, misses the fact that he is also a victim who is quite literally "caught" and sacrificed in a scene that echoes a public ritual.

## CHAPTER 2.
### *HEART OF DARKNESS:* OUTSIDER DEMYSTIFIED

1. See René Girard's discussion of primitive taboos against twins in *Violence and the Sacred.* As Girard argues, the blurring of physical distinctions associated with twins must, in primitive societies, be defended against because it portends the breakdown of the foundational distinctions upon which the stability of such societies depends: "The disappearance of natural differences can thus bring to mind the dissolution of regulations pertaining to the individual's proper place in society—that is, can instigate a sacrificial crisis" (56).

2. Peter Brooks has written the classic analysis of the repeated tellings and readings of Marlow's story. However, his emphasis on the resulting indeterminacy, while certainly valid, misses the fact that these successive readings are, according to the logic of the novel itself, oriented toward an ultimately transparent, non-sacrificial reading (which, to be sure, will never be entirely achieved).

3. Achebe's essay, first published in 1977, continues to provoke spirited dissent within the Conrad community. My own view is that, even if some of Achebe's individual observations are questionable (especially the ad hominem attacks that he mounts against Conrad and Marlow), his core contention—that the plot of the novel is generated by an underlying sacrificial mechanism—is correct. Failure to recognize scapegoating as the motive underlying the narrative logic of *Heart of Darkness* vitiates Peter Firchow's attempt to deal dismissively with Achebe's critique. Firchow insists that Conrad cannot be faulted for his inaccurate portrayal of Africa since his goal was not to describe Africa as it really is but, rather, to present an "image" of Africa; in his subsequent discussion of this doubtlessly valid point, however, he entirely misses the ideological, scapegoating purpose that this image serves within the novel. As a result he is puzzled by the fact that Marlow describes Kurtz as being "alone" when he is, as Firchow observes, "very much in the company of the Black Amazon and his African followers" (*Envisioning Africa,* 119). As the scapegoating hypothesis allows us to see, however, there is no contradiction in Marlow's discovering, in that "blank space" reserved for the scapegoat, both a *group* of cannibals and a *solitary* European. They represent, respectively, the primitive community and the deracinated artist/intellectual whose "sacrifice" his narrative enacts.

4. For an intriguing discussion of the apparent homophobia of Marlow's listeners see Donald S. Wilson's "The Beast in the Congo: How Victorian Homophobia Inflects Marlow's *Heart of Darkness.*" Wilson's argument that the homosexual is implicitly a figure who must be banished from the "already hermetically sealed nexus of male privilege" (97) suggests yet a further manifestation of the underlying scapegoating mechanism. He also posits a homoerotic element in the desire

that leads Marlow onward to Kurtz, an element to which Marlow can allude only covertly so as not to arouse the ire of his "conservative, homophobic, white, male audience" (107).

5. One of the best discussions of Marlow as the victim of Conrad's irony and the significance of this for future readings of *Heart of Darkness* appears in Sung Ryol Kim's essay, "Witness to Death: Marlow in The Heart of Darkness." Kim argues, in particular, that "[p]art of the challenge for the reader is to be aware of Marlow's contradictions and inconsistencies as he struggles to understand and to come to terms with what he has witnessed. Marlow himself is unwittingly a victim of irony in a novel filled with ironies. It is only after many rereadings that the reader discovers not only the significance of 'trifling' events but also glimpses the subtle shades of irony. This process of discovery, of seeing through the many-layered ironies, is not a purely intellectual exercise, for it entails moral apprehension on both Marlow's and the reader's part" (60).

## CHAPTER 3.
## BORROWED DESIRE IN *THE GOOD SOLDIER*

1. See, in this respect, Thomas Moser's fascinating discussion of Ford's own desire to "become" his friend, the aristocratic Arthur Marwood. Moser claims that Ford's novel *Mr. Fleight* can be read as "his pledge of allegiance to Marwood, as his longing, even, to *be* Marwood" (*Life in the Fiction*, 113). He also suggests that, in *Parade's End*, which he wrote after Marwood's death, Ford "split into Marwood, a real, if dead, person, who he could never be" (149).

2. For purposes of this discussion, I am only assuming that Edward experiences his desire for Nancy Rufford as something like an incestuous passion, a hypothesis that is clearly substantiated by the use of phrases like "taboo" and the "unthinkable thing." For a highly speculative attempt to prove the far more startling thesis that Nancy really is Edward's illegitimate daughter, see Dewey Ganzel, "What the Letter Said: Fact and Inference in *The Good Soldier*.")

3. I am indebted for this interpretation of Paolo and Francesca's predicament to René Girard's discussion of this episode in *Critique dans un souterrain*.

4. Bruce Bassoff suggests that Dowell's readiness to see signs of imitative behavior in his characters is, at least in part, a reflection of his own personality: "as a sentimentalist unable to see things for what they are, he exaggerates the others' tendency to talk like a book; as a man who has no self except the one which he acquires through Florence and the one with which he identifies in Edward Ashburnham, he exaggerates the others' tendency to elicit their 'characters' from each other" ("Oedipal Fantasy," 40). Bassoff also recognizes, however, that Dowell does not entirely invent these mimetic tendencies. Thus, he identifies Edward with Don Quixote because "he learns to be himself by learning to be a character in a book," a trait that is clearly in evidence when, for example, expressing "what is presumably his deepest anguish, he seems to be repeating lines written for him by someone else" (41).

5. This is not, however, to ignore the possibility, raised by several critics, that there really is, in *The Good Soldier*, a true story that Dowell is trying to keep hidden for perfectly self-interested reasons. In "Poor Florence Indeed! or: *The Good Soldier* Retold," for example, John Reichert offers the shocking (and perhaps not seriously intended) hypothesis that Dowell has both poisoned Florence and slit Edward's throat. Whether or not one accepts this theory, there is no difficulty in agreeing with the idea that Dowell has constructed for himself, not only a listener who is reliably "sympathetic," but a story that—notwithstanding, and perhaps even because of, its tragic aspects—is precisely the story that he *wants* to tell to such a listener.

6. For an interesting discussion of this point see Nigro, "Who Framed *The Good Soldier?*" 386–90.

## CHAPTER 4.
### *THE GREAT GATSBY*

1. A recent example of the nearly unanimous critical resistance to Hartley's lucidity is found in the chapter that Jeffrey Hart devotes to *Gatsby* in *Smiling Through the Cultural Catastrophe*. Arguing that "magical transformation" is the novel's true subject (230), Hart credits Nick with achieving an "epiphany" whereby he recognizes Gatsby's superiority to "the whole damn bunch put together" (238) and concludes that the larger significance of the novel rests with its affirmation that "the transforming imagination is immortal" (239).

2. The possibility of interpreting Nick's moral vision as the central feature of the novel was recognized from the beginning by Maxwell Perkins, Fitzgerald's editor, who, in his letter of 20 November 1924, praised the author for choosing a narrator "who is more of a spectator than an actor." According to Perkins, "[t]his puts the reader upon a point of observation on a higher level than that on which the characters stand" (Kuehl and Bryer, *Dear Scott/Dear Max*, 82). J. S. Westbrook develops this idea by attributing a central structural significance to Nick's point of view in his argument that "[t]o understand the unity of *The Great Gatsby* we must first recognize that its primary subject is the growth of an awareness. The awareness belongs to the narrator, Nick Carraway, who not only enjoys the advantages of distance in time from the events he relates, but even at the scene of their unfolding has been more of a perceiver than a protagonist" (in Claridge, *F. Scott Fitzgerald*, 265).

3. For an intelligent, although, in my view, not finally persuasive defense of Nick as a reliable narrator whose growth in moral judgment is the novel's true center, see E. Fred Carlisle, "The Triple Vision of Nick Carraway." Jeffrey Hart comes to a similarly positive conclusion about Nick's development. For Hart, Nick, who had appeared to be irredeemably "banal" throughout the novel, is "moved to completely unexpected eloquence . . . an operatic prose aria" in the novel's concluding paragraphs, an achievement that Hart interprets as proving that "[t]his new and lyrical Nick must have found his voice only through his total experience of Jay Gatsby" (*Smiling*, 238–39).

4. Frances Kerr offers an intriguing and well-argued analysis of the gender anxiety (in particular, the fear of having his romantic, feminine side exposed) that Nick displaces upon Gatsby. She then usefully describes the climactic scene in the Plaza Hotel as one in which Gatsby "is publicly feminized by Tom Buchanan" ("Feeling 'Half-Feminine,'"418), without, however, relating these insights to the underlying scapegoating pattern to which they point.

5. This point is missed by David H. Zimmerman in his otherwise valuable analysis of Gatsby in relation to the "monomyth" described by Joseph Campbell. While successfully setting Gatsby's own adventures against the tripartite stages of this myth—departure, initiation, and return—he ignores, in the midst of this mythic reading, the fact that the novel is actually a modern reenactment of an ancient scapegoating ritual. His focus on the individual hero scants the equally important role played by the community in performing this ceremony.

## CHAPTER 5.
## ENDING RITUALS

1. See Christine Froula, "St. Virginia's Epistle to an English Gentleman; or Sex, Violence, and the Public Sphere in Woolf's *Three Guineas*," for an excellent analysis, based on the theories of René Girard, of scapegoating practices as applied specifically to women.

2. Jane Lilienfeld, ignoring Woolf's ambivalence on this point, attributes this fear exclusively to such self-interested male figures as Sir Leslie Stephen, for whom "the family was both the crystalline form of all cultural bonding and the specific mode of order imposed on civilization." She then credits Woolf with unproblematically "smash[ing] the patriarchal super-structure of marriage as Leslie Stephen enforced it, and rework[ing] the emotional mode of the marriage bond." See "Where the Spear Plants Grew: the Ramsays' Marriage in *To the Lighthouse*" (in Marcus, *New Feminist Essays*, 148–69).

3. On this point, Christine Froula offers an illuminating discussion of the rationale that underlies Woolf's otherwise self-contradictory readiness to exclude working-class women from her Outsider's Society. According to Froula the distinctions that justify this exclusion "are perhaps most clearly understood as pragmatic rather than exclusionary in spirit. Woolf, that is, appeals to professional women because she views a measure of economic independence as a necessary precondition for the experimental work against barbarism and was for which women's historical experience as masculine culture's scapegoats has particularly fitted them; it is they who can best afford to use the social power of their newly emerging economic class to fight tyranny and collective violence" ("St. Virginia's Epistle," 41).

4. This interpretation is in accord with Tremper's choice of "fraternity" to describe Lily's achievement. See "In Her Father's House: *To the Lighthouse* as a Record of Virginia Woolf's Literary Patrimony." It is, however, in strong disagreement with an important line of interpretation of the novel which credits Lily with having destroyed male mediation. See, for example, Val Gough's discussion of the shift from

what he calls "phallic" to "mystical" copulas (in Hussey, *Emerging Perspectives*), Lilienfeld's choice of "selfhood" to describe the alternative to paternal bonding that she believes Lily achieves, and Tina Barr's argument, in "Divine Politics: Virginia Woolf's Journey toward Eleusis in *To the Lighthouse*," that Lily's completion of her painting implies the replacement of the father/son bond by the mother/daughter bond.

5. For a comprehensive and insightful discussion of the relationship between Lily's painting and the impressionist and postimpressionist movements, see Jane Goldman's *The Feminist Aesthetics of Virginia Woolf.*

6. In this respect, Virginia Hyman, in "Reflections in the Looking-Glass: Leslie Stephen and Virginia Woolf," makes a relevant observation concerning Woolf's own tendency in her later life to diminish the importance of her father: as a result, "the father, whom she had begun by emulating, became increasingly the figure whom she most wished to deny, for he had bequeathed to her a heritage that was both admirable and threatening."

7. See, for example, Joan Lidoff, "Virginia Woolf's Feminine Sentence: The Mother-Daughter World of *To the Lighthouse*" and Tina Barr, "Divine Politics."

8. In *"To the Lighthouse": The Marriage of Life and Art,* Alice van Buren Kelley suggests the origin in Woolf's own life of this aspect of Lily's situation when she remarks that "Virginia Woolf faced a formidable challenge in attempting to create a novel that was a work of art, surrounded as she was by men of such firm opinion, whose theories she both admired and, in good part, shared. Yet it is clear that she saw in the best literature just those elements of purified reality, set beyond the limits of mere representation, that Fry and Bell found in the best paintings" (69).

9. This interpretation of the significance of Carmichael's fraternal role contrasts with interpretations that view Lily's achievement in completing her painting as implying a rejection of the priority of the fraternal bond. A good example of this latter view is presented by Diana Swanson, who contends that "Through the figure of Antigone, Woolf rewrites psychoanalytical theories of the female Oedipus complex to include the daughter's struggle for self-respect and self-determination and her desire for liberty, that is, her own particular quest for subjecthood. This daughter's quest holds great potential for social change whereas the son's rebellion against the father, as delineated in the Oedipus complex, does not result in a challenge to the patriarchal social system." "An Antigone Complex? The Political Psychology of *The Years* and *Three Guineas*," *Woolf Studies Annual 3* (1997): 29–30.

# Bibliography

Abbott, H. Porter. "Character and Modernism: Reading Woolf Writing Woolf." *New Literary History* 24 (spring 1993): 393–405.

Aldrich, C. Knight. "Another Twist to *The Turn of the Screw*." *Modern Fiction Studies* 13 (summer 1967): 167–78.

Andera, Cesáreo. *The Sacred Game: The Role of the Sacred in the Genesis of Modern Literary Fiction*. University Park: Pennsylvania State University Press, 1994.

Anderson, Hilton. "Fitzgerald and the War Novel." *Publications of the Mississippi Philological Association* (1987): 143–53.

Armstrong, Paul B. "History and Epistemology: The Example of *The Turn of the Screw*." *New Literary History* 19 (spring 1988): 693–712.

Bailin, Miriam. " 'An Extraordinarily Safe Castle': Aesthetics as Refuge in *The Good Soldier*." *Modern Fiction Studies* 30 (winter 1984): 621–36.

Barge, Laura. "René Girard's Categories of Scapegoats and the Literature of the South." *Christianity and Literature* 50 (winter 2001): 247–68.

Barr, Tina. "Divine Politics: Virginia Woolf's Journey to Eleusis in *To the Lighthouse*." *Boundary 2* 20 (spring 1993): 125–45.

Bassoff, Bruce. "Drifting with Henry James." *Reader: Essays in Reader-Oriented Theory, Criticism and Pedagogy* 17 (spring 1987): 44–57.

———."Oedipal Fantasy and Arrested Development in *The Good Soldier*." *Twentieth Century Literature* 34 (spring 1998): 40–47.

Beidler, Peter, ed. *"The Turn of the Screw": A Case Study in Contemporary Criticism*. New York: St. Martin's Press, 1995.

Bell, Ian F. A., ed. *Henry James: Fiction as History*. New York: Vision and Barnes & Noble, 1984.

Bell, Michael. *Literature, Modernism and Myth: Belief and Responsibility in the Twentieth Century*. Cambridge: Cambridge University Press, 1997.

Bell, Millicent. *Meaning in Henry James*. Cambridge: Harvard University Press, 1991.

Bloom, Harold. *Virginia Woolf's "To the Lighthouse"*. New York: Chelsea House, 1988.

Bode, Rita. " 'They . . . Should Be Out of It': The Women of *Heart of Darkness*." *Conradiana* 26 (spring 1994): 20–34.

Boehm, Beth A. "A Postmodern Turn of *The Turn of the Screw*." *The Henry James Review* 19 (fall 1998): 245–54.

Brivic, Sheldon. "Love as Destruction in Woolf's *To the Lighhouse*." *Mosaic* 27 (September 1994): 65–85.

Brooks, Peter. *Reading for the Plot: Design and Intention in Narrative*. New York: Knopf, 1984.

Brown, Tony C. "Cultural Psychosis on the Frontier: The Work of the Darkness in Joseph Conrad's *Heart of Darkness*." *Studies in the Novel* 32 (spring 2000): 14–28.

Bruccoli, Matthew J., ed. *New Essays on "The Great Gatsby*." Cambridge: Cambridge University Press, 1985.

Bryer, Jackson R., Alan Margolies, and Ruth Prigozy, eds. *F. Scott Fitzgerald: New Perspectives*. Athens: University of Georgia Press, 2000.

Carlisle, E. Fred. "The Triple Vision of Nick Carraway." *Modern Fiction Studies* 11 (winter 1965): 351–60.

Carter, C. Allen. *Kenneth Burke and the Scapegoat Process*. Norman: University of Oklahoma Press, 1997.

Cartwright, Kent. "Nick Carraway as an Unreliable Narrator." *Papers on Language and Literature* 20 (spring 1984): 218–32.

Cassell, Richard, ed. *Critical Essays on Ford Madox Ford*. Boston: Twayne, 1987.

Caws, Mary Ann. "Framing in Two Opposite Modes: Ford and Wharton." *Comparatist* 10 (May 1986): 114–20.

Cheng, Vincent J. "Religious Differences in *The Good Soldier*: The 'Protest' Scene." *Renascence* 37 (summer 1985): 238–47.

———. "The Spirit of *The Good Soldier* and *The Spirit of the People*." *English Literature in Transition* 32, no.3 (1989): 303–16.

Christensen, Bryce J. "The Mystery of Ungodliness: Renan's *Life of Jesus* as a Subtext for Fitzgerald's *The Great Gatsby* and 'Absolution.'" *Christianity and Literature* 36 (fall 1986): 15–23.

Claridge, Henry, ed. *F. Scott Fitzgerald: Critical Assessment*. East Sussex: Helm Information, 1991.

Clayton, John J. *Gestures of Healing: Anxiety and the Modern Novel*. Amherst: University of Massachusetts Press, 1991.

Cleary, Thomas and Terry Sherwood. "Women in Conrad's Ironical Epic: Virgil, Dante and *Heart of Darkness*." *Conradiana* 16 (Autumn 1984): 183–94.

Coleman, Hildy. "The Actual and the Notional in *The Great Gatsby*: A Topographical Survey." *ANQ* 4 (July 1991): 132–34.

Conrad, Joseph. *Selected Literary Criticism and "The Shadow-Line*." Edited by Allan Ingram. London: Methuen, 1986.

———. *Heart of Darkness*. New York: Penguin, 1995.

Cornwell, Neil, and Maggie Malone, eds. *"The Turn of the Screw" and "What Maisie Knew": New Critical Essays*. New York: St. Martin's Press, 1998.

Crowl, Susan. "Aesthetic Allegory in *The Turn of the Screw.*" *Novel* 4 (winter 1971): 107–22.

Curtsinger, E. C. "*The Turn of the Screw* as Writer's Parable." *Studies in the Novel* 12 (winter 1980): 344–58.

Dante [Alighieri]. *Inferno*. Trans. Allen Mandelbaum. Berkeley and Los Angeles: University of California Press, 1980.

Daugherty, Beth Rigel. *Virginia Woolf: Texts and Contexts*. New York: Pace University Press, 1996.

Daugherty, Beth Rigel and Mary Pringle, eds. *Approaches to Teaching Virginia Woolf's "To the Lighthouse."* New York: MLA, 2001.

DeKoster, Katie, ed. *Readings on F. Scott Fitzgerald*. San Diego: Greenhaven, 1998.

Dewey, Joseph, and Brooke Horvath, eds. "*The Finer Thread, The Tighter Weave*": *Essays on the Short Fiction of Henry James*. West Lafayette, Ind.: Purdue University Press, 2001.

Dickstein, Morris. "Fitzgerald's Second Act." *South Atlantic Quarterly*. 90 (summer 1991): 555–78.

Dillon, Andrew. "*The Great Gatsby*: The Vitality of Illusion." *Arizona Quarterly* 44 (spring 1988): 49–61.

Donaldson, Sandra. "Where does Q Leave Mr. Ramsay?" *Tulsa Studies in Women's Literature* 11 (fall 1992): 329–36.

Donaldson, Scott, ed. *Critical Essays on F. Scott Fitzgerald's "The Great Gatsby."* Boston: G. K. Hall, 1984

Douglas, Tom. *Scapegoats: Transferring Blame*. London: Routledge, 1995.

Dreiser, Theodore. "The Saddest Story." *The New Republic* 3 (12 June 1915): 155–56.

Dry, Helen Aristar and Susan Kucinkas. "Ghostly Ambiguity: Presuppositional Constructions in *The Turn of the Screw.*" *Style* 25 (spring 1991): 71–88.

Engelberg, Edward. *Solitude and Its Ambiguities in Modernist Fiction*. New York: Palgrave, 2001.

Erdinast-Vulcan, Daphna. *Joseph Conrad and the Modern Temper*. Oxford: Clarendon Press, 1991.

Esch, Debora, and Jonathan Warren, eds. "*The Turn of the Screw*": *A Norton Critical Edition*. New York: W. W. Norton & Co., 1999.

Fahey, William. "Fitzgerald's Eggs of Columbus." *ANQ*. 8 (fall 1995): 26–27.

Ferguson, John. "A Sea Change: Thomas de Quincy and Mr. Carmichael in *To the Lighthouse. Journal of Modern Literature* 14 (summer 1987): 45–63.

Fetterley, Judith. *The Resisting Reader: A Feminist Approach to American Fiction*. Bloomington: Indiana University Press, 1978.

Firchow, Peter. *Envisioning Africa: Racism and Imperialism in Conrad's "Heart of Darkness."* Lexington: University Press of Kentucky, 2000.

Fish, Stanley, *Surprised by Sin: The Reader in Paradise Lost*. Berkeley and Los Angeles: University of California Press, 1971.

Fitzgerald, F. Scott. *The Great Gatsby*. New York: Scribner, 1995.

Fleishman, Avrom. "The Genre of *The Good Soldier*: Ford's Comic Mastery." 41–53 in Bites, Jack I., ed. *British Novelists since 1900*. New York: AMS Press, 1987.

Fleming, Bruce. "Floundering about in Silence: What the Governess Couldn't Say." *Studies in Short Fiction* 26 (spring 1989): 135–43.

Ford, Ford Madox. *The Good Soldier*. New York: Vintage Books, 1989.

Foss, Chris. "Abjection and Appropriation: Male Subjectivity in *The Good Soldier*." *Literature* 9 (December 1998): 225–44.

Fraser, Robert, ed. *Sir James Frazer and the Literary Imagination: Essays in Affinity and Influence*. New York: St. Martin's Press, 1990.

Freedman, Jonathan. *The Cambridge Companion to Henry James*. Cambridge: Cambridge University Press, 1998.

Froula, Christine. "St. Virginia's Epistle to an English Gentleman; or Sex, Violence, and the Public Sphere in Woolf's *Three Guineas*." *Tulsa Studies in Women's Literature* 13 (spring 1994): 27–56.

Gans, Eric. *Signs of Paradox: Irony, Resentment and Other Mimetic Structures*. Palo Alto, Calif.: Stanford University Press, 1997.

Ganzel, Dewey. "What the Letter Said: Fact and Inference in *The Good Soldier*." *Journal of Modern Literature* 11 (July 1984): 277–90.

Gill, David. "The Fascination of the Abomination: Conrad and Cannibalism." *Conradian* 24 (autumn 1999): 1–30.

Gillespie, Diane Filby. *The Sister Arts: The Writing and Painting of Virginia Woolf and Vanessa Bell*. Syracuse, N.Y.: Syracuse University Press, 1988.

Girard, René. *Deceit, Desire and the Novel*. Trans. Yvonne Freccero. Baltimore: Johns Hopkins University Press, 1965.

———. *Critique dans un souterrain*. Paris: Grasset, 1976.

———. *Violence and the Sacred*. Trans. Patrick Gregory. Baltimore: Johns Hopkins University Press, 1977.

———. *The Scapegoat*. Trans. Yvonne Freccero. Baltimore: Johns Hopkins University Press, 1989.

———. *Things Hidden Since the Foundation of the World*. Trans. Stephen Bann and Michael Metteer. Palo Alto, Calif.: Stanford University Press, 1993.

Glenn, Ian. "Conrad's *Heart of Darkness*: A Sociological Reading." *Literature & History* 13 (Autumn 1987): 238–56.

Goldman, Jane. *The Feminist Aesthetics of Virginia Woolf*. Cambridge: Cambridge University Press, 1998.

Goodhart, Sandor. *Sacrificing Commentary*. Baltimore: Johns Hopkins University Press, 1996.

Gould, Eric. *Mythical Intentions in Modern Literature*. Princeton: Princeton University Press, 1981.

Graham, Wendy. *Henry James's Thwarted Love*. Palo Alto, Calif.: Stanford University Press, 1999.

Green, Michael. "*The Great Gatsby*: The Structure of the Dream." *CRUX: A Journal on the Teaching of English*. 22 (April 1988): 51–60.

Green, Robert. "'The Exploded Traditions' of Ford Madox Ford." *ELH* 48 (spring 1981): 217–30.

Guerard, Albert. *Conrad the Novelist.* Cambridge: Harvard University Press, 1962.

Guidin, James. "Politics in Contemporary Woolf Criticism." *Modern Language Quarterly* 47 (December 1988): 422–32.

Hadley, Tessa. *Henry James & The Imagination of Pleasure.* Cambridge: Cambridge University Press, 2002.

Hallab, Mary Y. "The Governess and the Demon Lover: The Return of a Fairy Tale." *The Henry James Review* 8 (winter 1987): 104–15.

Hamner, Robert D., ed. *Joseph Conrad: Third World Perspectives.* Washington, D.C.: Three Continents, 1990.

Hanzo, Thomas A. "The Theme of the Narrator in *The Great Gatsby.*" *Modern Fiction Studies* 2 (winter 1956–57): 183–90.

Hart, Jeffrey. "Anything Can Happen: Magical Transformation in *The Great Gatsby.*" *South Carolina Review* 25 (spring 1993): 37–50.

———. *Smiling through the Cultural Catastrophe: Toward the Revival of Higher Education.* New Haven: Yale University Press, 2001.

Haule, James. "'Le Temps Passe' and the Original Typescript." *Twentieth Century Literature* 29 (fall 1983): 267–311.

Hays, Peter. "*Nostromo* and *The Great Gatsby.*" *Etudes Anglaises* 41 (October–December 1988): 405–17.

Heilbrun, Carolyn. "Virginia Woolf in Her Fifties." *Twentieth Century Literature* 27 (spring 1981): 16–33.

Heyns, Michiel. *Expulsion and the Nineteenth-Century Novel.* Oxford: Clarendon Press, 1994.

Hochman, Barbara. "Dismembered Voices and Narrating Bodies in *The Great Gatsby.*" *Style* 28 (spring 1994): 95–118.

Hoffmann, Charles. *Ford Madox Ford.* Boston: Twayne, 1990.

Hood, Richard A. "'Constant Reduction': Modernism and the Narrative Structure of *The Good Soldier.*" *Journal of Modern Literature* 14 (spring 1988): 445–64.

Hoople, Robin P. *Distinguished Discord: Discontinuity & Pattern in the Critical Tradition of "The Turn of the Screw."* Lewisburg, Pa.: Bucknell University Press, 1997.

Humphries, Reynold. "The Discourse of Colonialism: Its Meaning and Relevance for Conrad's Fiction." *Conradiana* 21 (summer 1989): 107–33.

———. ed. *Seduction & Theory: Readings of Gender, Representation, and Rhetoric.* Urbana: University of Illinois Press, 1989.

Hunter, Dianne. "Taking the Figurative Literally: Language and *Heart of Darkness.*" *Etudes Anglaises* 46 (January–March 1993): 19–31.

Hussey, Mark, ed. *Virginia Woolf and War: Fiction, Reality and Myth.* Syracuse, N.Y.: Syracuse University Press, 1991.

———, ed. *Virginia Woolf: Emerging Perspectives.* New York: Pace University Press, 1994.

Hyland, Peter. "The Little Woman in *Heart of Darkness.*" *Conradiana* 20 (spring 1988): 3–11.

Hyman, Virginia R. "Reflections in the Looking Glass." *Journal of Modern Literature* 10 (June 1983): 197–216.

Jacobs, Carol. "The (Too) Good Soldier: A Real Story." *Glyph* 3 (spring 1978): 32–51.

James, Henry. *The Aspern Papers and The Turn of the Screw.* New York: Penguin, 1985.

Johnsen, William A. "The Sparagmos of Myth is the Naked Lunch of Mode: Modern Literature as the Age of Frye and Borges." *Boundary* 2 8 (fall 1980): 297–311.

———. "René Girard and the Boundaries of Modern Literature." *Boundary 2* 9 (winter 1981): 277–93.

———. The Moment of *The American* in l'Ecriture Judéo-Chrétienne." *The Henry James Review* 5 (spring 1984): 216–20.

———. "Ibsen's Drama of Self-Sacrifice." *Contagion* 3 (spring 1996): 1–20.

Judd, Alan. *Ford Madox Ford.* Cambridge: Harvard University Press, 1991.

Kaplan, Carola M. "Colonizers, Cannibals and the Horror of Good Intentions in Joseph Conrad's *Heart of Darkness.*" *Studies in Short Fiction* 34 (summer 1997): 323–33.

Kearney, Richard. "Myths and Scapegoats: The Case of René Girard." *Theory, Culture and Society* 12 (November 1995): 1–12.

Kelley, Alice van Buren. *"To the Lighthouse": The Marriage of Life and Art.* Boston: Twayne Publishers, 1987.

Kerr, Francis. "Feeling 'Half-Feminine': Modernism and the Politics of Emotion in *The Great Gatsby.*" *American Literature* 68 (June 1996): 405–31.

Ketterer, David. "'Griffin': One-Upping and an H. G. Wells Allusion in *The Turn of the Screw.*" *English Studies in Canada* 26 (June 2000): 180–92.

Killoran, Helen. "The Governess, Mrs. Grose and 'the Poison of an Influence' in *The Turn of the Screw.*" *Modern language Studies* 23 (spring 1993): 13–24.

Kim, Sung Ryol. "Witness to Death: Marlow in The Heart of Darkness. *Conradiania* 33 (spring 2001): 59–77.

Kimbrough, Robert, ed. *"Heart of Darkness": An Authoritative Text, Backgrounds and Sources, Criticism.* New York: W. W. Norton & Co., 1988.

Knapp, Bettina. "Virginia Woolf's Boeuf en Daube." in *Literary Gastronomy,* ed. David Beran, 29–36. Amsterdam: Rodopi, 1988.

Kohan, Kevin. "James and the Originary Scene." *The Henry James Review* 22 (fall 2001): 229–38.

Kratter, Matthew. "'Christ Follows Dionysus': Myth, Modernism, and the Mimetic Theory of René Girard." Ph.D. diss., University of California, Berkeley, 2000.

Krumrey, Ami M. "Nick Carraway's Process of Individuation." *Journal of Evolutionary Psychology* 15 (August 1994): 249–58.

Kuehl, John, and Jackson R. Bryer. *Dear Scott/Dear Max: The Fitzgerald-Perkins Correspondence.* New York: Scribner, 1971.

Kunat, John. "The Function of Augustus Carmichael in Virginia Woolf's *To the Lighthouse.*" *Xanadu: A Literary Journal* 13 (1990): 48–59.

Leavis, F. R. *The Great Tradition*. New York: New York University Press, 1963.

Lee, A. Robert, ed. *Scott Fitzgerald: The Promises of Life*. London: Visions Press, 1989.

Lee, Hermione. *The Novels of Virginia Woolf*. London: Metheun, 1977.

Lehan, Richard. *The Great Gatsby: The Limits of Wonder*. Boston: G. K. Hall, 1989.

Levenson, Michael. "Character in *The Good Soldier*. *Twentieth Century Literature* 30 (winter 1984): 373–87.

———, ed. *The Cambridge Companion to Modernism*. Cambridge: Cambridge University Press, 1999.

LeVot, André. *F. Scott Fitzgerald: A Biography*. Boston: Warner Books, 1984.

Levy, Eric. "Woolf's Metaphysics of Tragic Vision in *To the Lighthouse*." *Philological Quarterly* 75 (winter 1996): 109–32.

Lewis, Pericles. "'His Sympathies Were in the Right Place': *Heart of Darkness* and the Discourse of National Character." *Nineteenth-Century Literature* 53 (September 1998): 211–44.

Lidoff, Joan. "Virginia Woolf's Feminine Sentence: The Mother-Daughter World of *To the Lighthouse*." *Literature and Psychology* 32, no. 3 (1986): 43–59.

Lilienfeld, Jane. *Reading Alcoholisms: Theorizing Character and Narrative in Selected Novels of Thomas Hardy, James Joyce, and Virginia Woolf*. New York: St. Martin's Press, 1999.

Lockridge, Ernest. "F. Scott Fitzgerald's Trompe l'oeil and *The Great Gatsby's* Buried Plot." *Journal of Narrative Theory* 17 (spring 1987): 163–83.

London, Bette. "Reading Race and Gender in Conrad's Dark Continent." *Criticism* 31 (summer 1989): 235–52.

Losey, Jay. "Moments of Awakening in Conrad's Fiction." *Conradiana* 20 (summer 1988): 89–108.

Ludwig, Richard M. *Letters of Ford Madox Ford*. Princeton: Princeton University Press, 1965.

Lukens, Margaret. "Gatsby as a Drowned Sailor." *The English Journal* 76 (February 1987): 44–48.

Lund, Roger D. "We Perished Each Alone: 'The Castaway' and *To the Lighthouse*." *Journal of Modern Literature* 16 (summer 1989): 75–92.

Ludwig, Sami. "Metaphors, Cognition and Behavior: The Reality of Sexual Puns in *The Turn of the Screw*." *Mosaic* 27 (March 1994): 33–53.

Lynn, David. "Watching the Orchards Robbed: Dowell and *The Good Soldier*." *Studies in the Novel* 16 (winter 1984): 410–23.

Mahbobah, Albaraq. "Hysteria, Rhetoric, and the Politics of Reversal in Henry James's *The Turn of the Screw*." *The Henry James Review* 17 (spring 1996): 149–61.

Marcus, Jane. *New Feminist Essays on Virginia Woolf*. Lincoln: University of Nebraska Press, 1981.

Martin, Bill. "*To the Lighthouse* and the Feminist Path to Postmodernity." *Philosophy and Literature* 13 (October 1989): 307–15.

Marwick, M. J. "Right and Wrong in *The Great Gatsby*." *CRUX* 20 (August 1986): 24–32.

McCarthy, Jeffrey. "*The Good Soldier* and the War for British Modernism." *Meddelanden fran Strindbergssallskapet* 45 (summer 1999): 303–39.

McCarthy, Patrick. "In Search of Lost Time: Chronology and Narration in *The Good Soldier*. *English Literature in Transition (1880–1920)* 40, no. 2 (1997): 133–49.

McCormack, Peggy. *Questioning the Master: Gender and Sexuality in Henry James's Writing*. Newark: University of Delaware Press, 2000.

McCune, Marjorie, Tucker Orbison, and Philip M Withim, eds. *The Binding of Proteus: Perspectives on Myth and the Literary Process*. Lewisburg, Pa.: Bucknell University Press, 1974.

McMaster, Graham. "Henry James and India: A Historical Reading of *The Turn of the Screw*." *Clio* 18, no. 1: 23–40.

Matheson, Neill. "Talking Horrors: James, Euphemism, and the Specter of Wilde." *American Literature* 71 (December 1999): 709–50.

McVicker, Jeanette, and Laura Davis, eds. *Virginia Woolf and Communities*. New York: Pace University Press, 1999.

May, Brian. "Ford Madox Ford and the Politics of Impressionism." *Essays in Literature* 21 (spring 1994): 82–96.

Meisel, Perry. "Decentering *Heart of Darkness*." *Modern Language Studies* 8, no. 3 (1978): 20–28.

Miall, David S. "Designed Horror: James's Vision of Evil in *The Turn of the Screw*." *Nineteenth-Century Literature* 39 (December 1984): 305–27.

Miller, J. Hillis. "Mr. Carmichael and Lily Briscoe" in *Modernism Reconsidered*, ed. Robert Kiely. Cambridge: Harvard University Press, 1983.

Mitchell, Giles. "The Great Narcissist: A Study of Fitzgerald's Jay Gatsby." *The American Journal of Psychoanalysis* 51 (December 1991): 387–96.

Mizner, Arthur. "*The Good Soldier*." *The Southern Review* 6 (1970): 589–602.

Mizruchi, Susan L. *The Science of Sacrifice: American Literature and Modern Social Theory*. Princeton: Princeton University Press, 1998.

———. "The Place of Ritual in our Time." *American Literary History* 12 (fall 2000): 467–92.

Moddelmog, Debra A. "Faulkner's Theban Saga: *Light in August*." *Southern Literary Journal* 18 (fall 1985): 13–29.

Monteiro, George. "Carraway's Complaint." *Journal of Modern Literature* 24 (fall 2000): 161–71.

Morgan, Elizabeth. "Gatsby in the Garden: Courtly Love and Irony." *College Literature* 11 (spring 1984): 163–77.

Moser, Thomas C. *The Life in the Fiction of Ford Madox Ford*. Princeton: Princeton University Press, 1980.

Mozina, Andrew. *Joseph Conrad and the Art of Sacrifice: The Evolution of the Scapegoat Theme in Joseph Conrad's Fiction*. New York: Routledge, 2001.

Murfin, Ross, ed. "*Heart of Darkness*": Case Studies in Contemporary Criticism. Boston: St. Martin's Press, 1996.

Newman, Beth. "Getting Fixed: Feminine Identity and Scopic Crisis in *The Turn of the Screw.*" *Novel: A Forum on Fiction* 26 (fall 1992): 43–63.

Nigro, Frank G. "Who Framed *The Good Soldier?* Dowell's Story in Search of a Form." *Studies in the Novel* 24 (winter 1992): 381–91.

Orr, Leonard and Ted Billy, eds. *A Joseph Conrad Companion.* Westport, Conn.: Greenwood, 1999.

Pauley, Thomas H. "Gatsby as Gangster." *Studies in American Fiction* 21 (autumn 1993): 225–36.

Pecora, Vincent. "*Heart of Darkness* and the Phenomenology of Voice." *ELH* 52 (winter 1985): 993–1015.

Petry, Alice Hall. "Jamesian Parody, *Jane Eyre*, and *The Turn of the Screw.*" *Modern Language Studies* 13 (fall 1983): 61–78.

Pippin, Robert B. *Henry James and Modern Moral Life.* Cambridge: Cambridge University Press, 2001.

Pollak, Vivian, ed. *New Essays on "Daisy Miller" and "The Turn of the Screw."* Cambridge: Cambridge University Press, 1993.

Poole, Roger. "The Real Plot Line of Ford Madox Ford's *The Good Soldier:* An Essay in Applied Deconstruction." *Textual Practice* 4 (winter 1990): 390–427.

Preston, Elizabeth. "Implying Authors in *The Great Gatsby. Narrative* 5 (May 1997): 143–64.

Reichert, John. "Poor Florence Indeed! or: *The Good Soldier* Retold." *Studies in the Novel* 14 (summer 1982): 161–79.

Rentz, Kathryn. "The Question of James's Influence on Ford's *The Good Soldier.*" *English Literature in Transition* 25 (1982): 104–14.

Rohrkemper, John. "The Allusive Past: Historical Perspective in *The Great Gatsby.*" *College Literature* 12 (spring 1985): 153–62.

Roth, Marty. "The Milk of Wonder: Fitzgerald, Alcoholism, and *The Great Gatsby. Dionysos* 2 (fall 1990): 3–10.

Rust, Richard. "Liminality in *The Turn of the Screw.*" *Studies in Short Fiction* 25 (fall 1988): 441–46.

Sawyer, Richard. "What's Your Title?—*The Turn of the Screw.*" *Studies in Short Fiction* 30 (winter 1993): 53–61.

Scott, James B. "Coincidence or Irony?; Ford's Use of August 4 in *The Good Soldier.*" *English Language Notes* 30 (June 1993): 53–58.

Scubla, Lucien. "Vindicatory System, Sacrificial System: From Opposition to Reconciliation." *Stanford French Review* 16 (1992): 55–76.

Segal, Robert A., ed. *Theories of Myth: From Ancient Israel and Greece to Freud, Jung, Campbell and Lévi-Strauss.* New York: Garland Publishing, Inc., 1996.

Sherry, Norman, ed. *Conrad: The Critical Heritage.* London: Routledge, 1973.

Silverman, Kaja. "Too Early/Too Late: Subjectivity and the Primal Scene in Henry James." *Novel: A Forum on Fiction* 21 (winter–spring 1988): 147–73.

Smith, Elton E. and Robert Haas. *The Haunted Mind: The Supernatural in Victorian Literature.* Lanham, Md.: Scarecrow Press, Inc, 1999.

Snitow, Ann Barr. *Ford Madox Ford and the Voice of Uncertainty.* Baton Rouge: Louisiana State University Press, 1984.

Sprinker, Michael. "Historicizing Henry James." *The Henry James Review* 5 (1984): 203–7.

Squier, Susan. "Mirroring and Mothering." *Twentieth Century Literature* 27 (fall 1981): 272–88.

Stampfl, Barry. "Marlow's Rhetoric of (Self-)Deception in *Heart of Darkness.*" *MFS: Modern Fiction Studies* 37 (summer 1992): 183–96.

Stang, Sondra J., ed. *The Presence of Ford Madox Ford: A Memorial Volume of Essays, Poems and Memoirs.* Philadelphia: University of Pennsylvania Press, 1981.

———., ed. *Ford Madox Ford. Antaeus* 56 (1986).

Stape, J. H., ed. *The Cambridge Companion to Joseph Conrad.* Cambridge: Cambridge University Press, 1996.

Staten, Henry. "Conrad's Mortal Word." *Critical Inquiry* 12 (summer 1986): 720–40.

Stewart, Jack. "A 'Need of Distance and Blue': Space, Color, and Creativity in *To the Lighthouse.*" *Twentieth Century Literature* 46 (spring 2000): 78–99.

Straus, Nina Pelikan. "The Exclusion of the Intended from Secret Sharing in Conrad's *Heart of Darkness.*" *Novel: A Forum on Fiction* 20 (winter 1987): 123–37.

Swanson, Diana. "An Antigone Complex? The Political Psychology of *The Years* and *Three Guineas.*" *Woolf Studies Annual* 3 (1997).

Swisher, Clarice, ed. Readings on *Heart of Darkness.* San Diego: Greenhaven, 1999.

Taylor, Michael J. H. "A Note on the First Narrator of *The Turn of the Screw.*" *American Literature* 53 (January 1982): 717–22.

Todorov, Tzvetan. "Knowledge in the Void: *Heart of Darkness.*" Trans. Walter C. Putnam III. *Conradiana* 21 (autumn 1989): 161–72.

Tratner, Michael. "Figures in the Dark: Working Class Women in *To the Lighthouse.*" *Virginia Woolf Miscellany* 40 (spring 1993): 3–4.

Tredell, Nicolas, ed. *F. Scott Fitzgerald: "The Great Gatsby."* New York: Columbia University Press, 1997.

———, ed. *Joseph Conrad: "Heart of Darkness."* New York: Columbia University Press, 1998.

Tremper, Ellen. "In Her Father's House: *To the Lighthouse* as a Record of Virginia Woolf's Literary Patrimony." *Texas Studies in Language and Literature* 34 (spring 1992): 1–40.

———. "The Earth of Our Earliest Life." *Journal of Modern Literature* 19 (summer 1994): 163–71.

Trench-Bonett, Dorothy. "Naming and Silence: A Study of Language and the Other in Conrad's *Heart of Darkness.*" *Conradiana* 32 (summer 2000): 84–95.

Turnbull, Andrew, ed. *The Letters of F. Scott Fitzgerald.* New York: Scribner, 1963.

Tuttleton, James W. "F. Scott Fitzgerald and the Magical Glory." *New Criterion* 13 (November 1994): 24–31.

Van Peer, Willie, and Ewout van der Knapp. "(In)Compatible Interpretations? Contesting Readings of *The Turn of the Screw.*" *Modern Language Notes* 110 (September 1995): 692–710.

Vickery, John. *The Literary Impact of "The Golden Bough."* Princeton: Princeton University Press, 1973.

Viola, André. "Fluidity versus Muscularity: Lily's Dilemma in Woolf's *To the Lighthouse.*" *Journal of Modern Literature* 24 (winter 2000/2001): 271–89.

Wasiolek, Edward. "The Sexual Drama of Nick and Gatsby." *The International Fiction Review* 19 (1992): 14–22.

Watson, Garry. "'The Fact and the Crucial Significance of Desire': Lawrence's 'Virgin and the Gipsy.'" *English* 34 (summer 1985): 131–56.

Watt, Ian. *Conrad in the Nineteenth Century.* Berkeley and Los Angeles: University of California Press, 1979.

————. *Essays on Conrad.* Cambridge: Cambridge University Press, 2000.

Watts, Cedric. *The Deceptive Text: An Introduction to Covert Plots.* Totowa, N.J.: Barnes and Noble Books, 1984.

Way, Brian. *F. Scott Fitzgerald and the Art of Social Fiction.* New York: St. Martin's Press, 1980.

Weston, Jessie. *From Ritual to Romance.* Garden City, N.Y.: Doubleday, 1957.

Whelan, Robert Emmet. "Ordinary Human Virture: The Key to *The Turn of the Screw.*" *Renascence* 40 (summer 1988): 247–67.

White, Patti. *Gatsby's Party.* West Lafayette, Ind.: Purdue University Press, 1992.

Williams, Jeff. "Narrative Games: The Frame of *The Turn of the Screw.*" *The Journal of Narrative Technique* 28 (winter 1998): 43–55.

Williams, Lisa. *The Artist as Outsider in the Novels of Toni Morrison and Virginia Woolf.* Westport, Conn.: Greenwood Press, 2000.

Wilson, Donald S. "The Beast in the Congo: How Victorian Homophobia Inflects Marlow's *Heart of Darkness.*" *Conradiana* 32 (summer 2000): 96–118.

Witkowsky, Peter. "Cranford Revisited: Ford's Debt to Mrs. Gaskell in *The Good Soldier.*" *Twentieth Century Literature* 44 (fall 1998): 291–305.

Woolf, Virginia. *To the Lighthouse.* New York: Harcourt, Brace, Jovanovitch, 1981.

Wussow, Helen, ed. *New Essays on Virginia Woolf.* Dallas: Contemporary Research, 1995.

Zaal, J. "*The Great Gatsby:* A New Way of Using the Great Conradian Vitality?" *Theoria* 58 (May 1982): 1–11.

Zimmerman, David. "Jay Gatsby Goes the Round: Joseph Campbell's Monomyth in *The Great Gatsby.*" *Journal of the American Studies Association of Texas* 24 (October 1993): 57–70.

# Index